D0264951

ABERDEEN FC
Miscellany

ABERDEEN FC
Miscellany

*Aberdeen Trivia,
History, Facts & Stats*

KEVIN STIRLING

ABERDEEN FC
Miscellany

All statistics, facts and figures are correct as of 5th May 2009

© Kevin Stirling

Kevin Stirling has asserted his rights in accordance with the Copyright, Designs and Patents Act 1988 to be identified as the author of this work.

Published By:
Pitch Publishing (Brighton) Ltd
A2 Yeoman Gate
Yeoman Way
Durrington
BN13 3QZ

Email: info@pitchpublishing.co.uk
Web: www.pitchpublishing.co.uk

First published 2009
Reprinted 2015, 2017

A catalogue record for this book is available from the British Library.

10-digit ISBN: 1-9054114-3-X
13-digit ISBN: 978-1-9054114-3-6

Printed and bound in India by Replika Press Pvt. Ltd.

To my mother Ethel Dora, who has
helped me without question for
more years than I care to remember...

FOREWORD BY JOE HARPER

Having played for Aberdeen for the best part of nine years, in two different spells, it is always a pleasure to read about the exploits of Aberdeen players through the years and some of the incredible events at Pittodrie. I always looked upon playing for a club like Aberdeen as a privilege rather than a career. When I arrived at the club for the first time in 1969, it was a new adventure for me.

Little did I know back then that I would enjoy two spells with a club that brought me my happiest memories as a professional footballer. I have experienced football on both sides of the border and it was a bit like 'coming home' when I joined Aberdeen for a second time in 1976. Although I was born and brought up in the west of Scotland, Aberdeen had become my team, and I was proud to have played a part in their fantastic history.

That brings me around to looking through Kevin Stirling's latest work; *Aberdeen FC Miscellany*. Once again, Kevin has captured some memorable moments in Aberdeen FC history and with so many new facts emerging from some far off times, his research into the club is second to none. Getting to know Kevin over these last few years, his knowledge on the club is quite incredible and that is apparent in his latest work on the Dons. I hope you enjoy reading about the Dons past and present as much as I did.

Joe Harper,
Aberdeen FC, 1969–72 & 1976–81

ACKNOWLEDGEMENTS

Thanks again to my wife Bernadette and children Joanne and young Kevin who have put up with my usual moans and groans as the hours put towards my latest tome began to pile up. Thanks again to Pitch Publishing and Dan Tester for his smooth approach to editing the final draft. Finally thanks to Aberdeen supporters everywhere; never lose the faith.

INTRODUCTION

Aberdeen FC Miscellany is a unique look at Aberdeen through the years and covers as many of the lesser known moments as the unforgettable highs. The club remain proud of the fact that they are the only Scottish side to have won two European trophies; a full and comprehensive honours list includes every trophy and title won in the club's history.

The perception that the Dons' first major trophy was the 1947 Scottish Cup is not entirely correct. The first 'national' success came in November 1904 when the fledgling Aberdeen were not even in the mainstream of the Scottish game. A Qualifying Cup win over Renton at Dens Park in Dundee, attracted the first ever substantial 'away' support as more than 1,500 left Aberdeen to attend the final, bedecked in the famous black and gold. In 1946, after the country was picking up the pieces following the end of the war, Aberdeen defeated Rangers in the Southern League Cup final.

With a new stadium on the horizon, Pittodrie will soon be consigned to history. The old ground has gone through many changes in 110 years and has been used for more than just football. Aberdeen have enjoyed some great players through the years and many have become part of Pittodrie folklore. While the likes of Joe Harper and Willie Miller are revered to this day, many of the lesser known players are also included for some remarkable feats.

Scoring six goals in any game is some achievement. Aberdeen have had two; Alex Merrie and Paddy Moore, the remarkable Irish forward. This book is all about the great players who have had the absolute privilege to wear the black and gold, and latterly the red, of Aberdeen, making their own contribution to the great history of the club.

Kevin Stirling, August 2009

'BEST PENALTY BOX DEFENDER IN THE WORLD'

The words of former Aberdeen boss Sir Alex Ferguson as he described his captain Willie Miller. The Aberdeen legend spent his entire professional career with the Dons after joining the club in 1971. He signed off his playing days with a second testimonial in 1990. In between times Miller led Aberdeen to unprecedented success at home and abroad. Miller captained the Dons to triumphs in the League Cup in 1976 and then Premier League titles, four Scottish FA Cups, two League Cups, and of course, the European Cup Winners' Cup and European Super Cup in 1983. Miller went on to coach the young Dons for a short spell before taking over as manager in February 1992. In 2004 Miller returned to the club as football director, a position he holds to the current day.

30 NOT OUT

Between February and December 1980, the Dons incredibly went 30 consecutive Premier League games unbeaten. After a shock 2-1 home defeat to Kilmarnock on February 23rd that year, the Dons went on to win the Premier that season which culminated in a 5-0 win against Hibernian at Easter Road on the final Saturday of the season. With Aberdeen looking to retain their title, they remained undefeated in their first 15 league games of the 1980-81 season to set a club, and Premier League, record. It was not until Morton beat Aberdeen on December 6th at Cappielow that Aberdeen would suffer another league defeat.

COLMAN'S DUGOUT

Pittodrie was the first ground in Britain to boast of having a conventional dugout, which remains a focal point of all stadia in the modern game. Aberdeen legend Donald Colman was behind the move in 1920. The Scotland international would spend his summer coaching in Norway and it was the inclement weather in that country that he took the idea from and brought it to Britain. Colman was always a keen student of the game and he was keen to watch player movements from 'ground level'. The first dugout was a basic shelter, but the term dugout was exactly that as the structure was excavated below ground level. Colman was previously a distinguished full back for Aberdeen and the oldest Don to be capped at the age of 33.

ABERDEEN LEGEND WILLIE MILLER

BLACKWELL'S BROLLY

Aberdeen defeated Highland League side Peterhead 13-0 in a Scottish Cup tie at Pittodrie on 10th February 1923 in what remains a club record score. Originally, Peterhead had home advantage but the 'Blue Toon' minnows were keen to switch the game to Pittodrie in the hope of attracting a big attendance. While they negotiated a deal with Aberdeen to surrender home advantage, this was all done without them consulting their players, who believed that they could create a shock. Giving up ground rights would make the task all the more difficult and when Peterhead announced that no bonus payments would be forthcoming they had a potential strike on their hands. As it was, several of the Peterhead first team refused to play and they were forced to draft in two Aberdeen University players under assumed names to be able to field eleven players. The farcical nature of the game took another twist when the Aberdeen area was hit with gales and lashing rain on the day of the game. The poor weather conditions meant that the anticipated large attendance never materialised and only 3,241 hardy souls were there to witness the Dons' record score. The result was hardly surprising given that the visitors were missing five first team players after the bonus dispute. The irony was that the tie would have more than likely attracted a larger gate had it been staged in Peterhead under more favourable conditions. As for the game it was effectively over after ten minutes as Aberdeen raced into a three-goal lead. Walter Grant opened the scoring in three minutes and Doug Thomson scored twice to end the resistance of the part-time visitors. Harry Blackwell was the Aberdeen keeper back then and he was well-known for his 'conversations' with supporters behind his goal during spells of inactivity. Against Peterhead, the Aberdeen custodian was, in effect, a spectator in the true sense as one sympathetic fan handed him an umbrella and waterproof coat to shield him from the elements! On only one occasion it was reported that Blackwell shed his protective gear to save from 'Allen', better known as J. T. Wiseman of Aberdeen University. A Vic Milne penalty and an Andy Rankine header put Aberdeen 5-0 ahead as the players returned to the relative comfort of the dressing room at half-time. By the time Aberdeen had completed the rout, two Peterhead players had left the field suffering from exposure. Ironically, Aberdeen lost out as they had to pay Peterhead a guarantee of £200 while only £181 was taken at the gate.

RECORD DEFEAT

Official records state that the Dons' record defeat was against Celtic at Parkhead in January 1965 in an 8-0 trouncing. In 1909 an Aberdeen first team were beaten 9-2 by Dundee in an Inter-City League match that was usually played between the competing sides' first XIs. However, it was on the day when Sir Winston Churchill was laid to rest on January 30th 1965 that Aberdeen succumbed to Celtic in a humiliating defeat. There was a doubt as to the game going ahead as the Glasgow pitch was hard and frost bound. While Aberdeen laboured in the conditions, Celtic winger John Hughes turned out in his training shoes and proceeded to cut through the Dons defence at will. Hughes went on to score five goals before a crowd of 14,000 at Parkhead. Ten days later Aberdeen manager Tommy Pearson resigned after the Dons were knocked out of the Scottish Cup by lowly East Fife.

THE WASPS

When Aberdeen Football Club came into being in April 1903, their first kit was an all-white one which not surprisingly led them to be known as 'The Whites'. A year later when Aberdeen were admitted into the Scottish League, the strip changed to their famous black and gold which remained unchanged until 1939. In those early days the club were nicknamed 'The Wasps' but the nickname was hugely unpopular with the players as it led to sarcastic quips from the terraces.

BON ACCORD

Better known as the city's slogan and is actually French for 'Good Agreement' it was used by Robert the Bruce in the 14th century as a password in the siege of Aberdeen Castle before destroying it in 1308, where he routed the English during the Scottish Wars of Independence to give the city back to the townspeople. In September 1885 a football team of the same name did not have as much resilience as they succumbed to a world record 36-0 defeat to Arbroath in a Scottish Cup tie. Their short and eventful existence lasted 11 games which ended in disgrace after their entire team walked off in a game against Aberdeen in February 1886 after disputing an Aberdeen goal.

THEY SHALL NOT PASS

Aberdeen hold a unique distinction when it comes to international keepers. In 1969, the regular Dons number one was Bobby Clark who was also a regular in the Scotland set up since earning his first full cap in 1967. With Aberdeen suffering two consecutive heavy defeats, Clark lost his place at Pittodrie to reserve keeper Ernie McGarr. Such was the impact made by McGarr that he was selected to play for Scotland against Ireland in Dublin on September 21st 1969. McGarr also played against Austria in November. By that time Clark had unsuccessfully tried his luck as an outfield player. Later that season Clark regained his place and was in goal for Scotland's next outing against Northern Ireland on April 18th 1970, a week after helping Aberdeen win the Scottish Cup. In 1954 Fred Martin, the Aberdeen keeper, was the first Scotland custodian to play in the World Cup finals in Switzerland. A year later the introduction of under-23 international football saw Aberdeen reserve keeper Reggie Morrison play for Scotland under-23s with Martin in the senior team. The feat was repeated in 1983 as Aberdeen's Jim Leighton was the regular international number one, while Dons reserve keeper Bryan Gunn was selected for the Scottish under-21 side.

HAMPDEN ROAR

Several theories have been put forward as to when the famous 'Hampden Roar' was first heard but the overwhelming school of thought was when Scotland played England at the old stadium in 1929. Playing on the right wing for Scotland that day was former Aberdeen legend and 'Wembley Wizard' Alec Jackson. At inside right was his former Aberdeen teammate Alec Cheyne who was still at Pittodrie. In the days before substitutes were allowed, Jackson broke an arm and the Scots were forced to play the entire second half with only ten men. Cheyne was asked to plough a lone furrow towards the English rearguard. With a minute remaining, the Aberdeen inside-forward walked over to take a rare corner for the Scots. Unknown to most of the 110,512 crowd, Cheyne had scored several goals for Aberdeen direct from corner kicks. Cheyne's corner deceived England keeper Hacking and flew into the far corner of the net to give Scotland the lead. The closing seconds were met with a crescendo of noise that saw Scotland through to victory and the 'Hampden Roar' was born.

'CUP-TIE MCKAY'

Not before or since has an Aberdeen player made such an impact as Derek McKay did in the side after emerging from relative obscurity to become a hero in 1970. Fate also played a part as McKay was brought into the Aberdeen first team for a crucial Scottish Cup quarter-final clash at Falkirk on February 21st 1970. A flu virus had decimated the Aberdeen squad and the SFA insisted that the game go ahead as Aberdeen could field eleven 'fit' players. Derek McKay had been a free-transfer signing from Dundee earlier that season. After scoring a sensational winner against Falkirk, McKay kept his place in the side for the semi-final against Kilmarnock and he once again scored the only goal of the game to take Aberdeen through to a Hampden final against Celtic. McKay scored the winner at Muirton Park, the former home of St. Johnstone in Perth. The fairytale was complete when McKay scored twice in a 3-1 win to take the Scottish Cup north for only the second time in the Dons' history. 'Cup-tie' as he became known by the Aberdeen support played on the right side of the Dons' three-pronged attack of pace and power that proved so effective against Celtic in the wide open spaces of Hampden. Months later McKay was released and he ended up moving to Australia where he remained until his untimely passing in 2008. Derek McKay only ever started 19 games for the club and his four goals all came in that cup run.

WALKING DOWN THE MERKLAND ROAD

A path trodden by generations of Aberdeen supporters on their way to Pittodrie; Merkland Road East is the access road off the main King Street in the city which leads to the stadium. The narrow street has been the scene of the thronging thousands in the 1940s and 1950s, through to some famous European nights at the old stadium. Recalled in song by the Red Army, Merkland Road remains part of Pittodrie folklore.

FIRST SCOTLAND CAP

Willie Lennie became the first Aberdeen player to represent Scotland when he was capped against Wales at Dens Park in Dundee on March 7th 1908. Lennie had been an outstanding winger for Aberdeen since joining the club in 1905 from Fulham. Lennie capped a memorable debut as he scored the winning goal in 87 minutes in the Scots' 2-1 win.

LET THERE BE LIGHT

Aberdeen were relatively late when it came to installing floodlights at Pittodrie. Although floodlit football was first known of in South America in the 1930s, it was not until the 1950s that most grounds in Britain followed suit. Aberdeen played in several 'floodlit friendlies' against English opponents as the days of Wednesday afternoon football were finished. It was not until 1959 that Pittodrie installed a new system. On October 21st 1959 Luton Town opened the new lights at Pittodrie as the Dons sported a new 'shiny' kit to go with their new surroundings. Two of those original pylons remain at the Merkland Road end of the ground today although the lights were changed in 1972 as Arbroath made use of the Dons' old system for their ground at Gayfield.

JUST NOT CRICKET

When the original Aberdeen Football Club came into being in October 1881, they were faced with securing use of a proper venue. Back then the Holburn Cricket Ground at the top of Holburn Street in the town was the only real recognised sporting facility in the area. Aberdeen played their first-ever home game there on April 15th 1882 when they lost 3-1 to Coupar Angus. The club had to compete with the established rugby and cricket teams for use of the ground and the Aberdeenshire Cricket Club in particular were difficult to deal with. Aberdeen later secured use of the grammar school grounds off Skene Street which allowed them to host Scottish Cup ties as the venue was classed as an enclosed ground and met cup regulations.

DONS PAY THE PENALTY

A first-ever shoot-out in Europe was hard for the Dons as they were knocked out of the ECWC after a dramatic penalty decider against Honved in Budapest. With both ties finishing 3-1 in favour of the home side, Aberdeen went into the new method of deciding European ties angered by a succession of poor decisions from the German officials. That continued throughout the penalties and after Jim Forrest struck the bar with his effort, Honved keeper Bickeci put the Hungarians through.

GREEK GIANTS

Orion is known in Greek mythology as a giant, and one of the founder-member clubs of Aberdeen FC certainly made their mark in their short history in the 19th century. Founded in 1885, the team from the northern agricultural part of the town played their first game on October 31st 1885, drawing 2-2 with Aberdeen. Orion went on to play out of their Central Park ground at Cattofield and were a fiercely ambitious club that went on to become Aberdeen's biggest rivals before they became part of the amalgamation process in 1903.

SINGING IN THE RAIN

Wednesday 11th May 1983is a date etched into Pittodrie folklore as it was on this night the Dons defeated the legendary Real Madrid to lift the ECWC. Goals from Eric Black and John Hewitt handed Aberdeen a famous 2-1 win over Madrid in extra time. More than 16,000 Aberdeen supporters made their way to Gothenburg in Sweden for the final. Weather conditions in the Swedish port were dreadful and on the day of the final the rain fell right up to the kick off. Conditions perhaps suited the Scots better and it was Aberdeen's superior fitness that helped them dominate the latter stages of the game. After the final whistle went it triggered ecstatic scenes with the Red Army singing in the rain and all through the night. The Aberdeen support made their way to the game by air, land and sea in all manner of transport.

DUNG HILL TO MUNITIONS DUMP

Pittodrie was originally a 'place of manure' which was used for the police horses in the town in the 19th century. Aberdeen Football Club took up the tenancy in 1899 and set about forming the ground that we know today. Dumbarton were the first visitors on September 2nd 1899 as Aberdeen officially opened the new ground. Alec Shiach had the distinction of scoring the first goal at the new ground. In 1900, the first international was played with a visit from Wales. Pittodrie has been used for many things through the years including being taken over by the Army during the Second World War and used as a munitions dump to aid the war effort.

KING STREET END

The Merkland Family Stand at Pittodrie was originally known as the King Street End and at one point was the only covered terraced area at Pittodrie. It allowed the Aberdeen songsters a home and a place to congregate for matches and was the scene of many passionate occasions and some memorable games at the old ground. That was in the days before any kind of segregation and the only seats that could be found were in the back of the Main Stand. In 1928 the granite facade that remains at Pittodrie today was built as a focal point for supporters coming down Merkland Road to the ground. In the 1970s the club fitted bench type seating in that area which was now called the 'Paddock' and that hastened a move away from the traditional end for many supporters. On October 9th 1985, for the visit of Dundee United in the League Cup semi-final, the new Merkland Stand was opened for the first time. The stand had been completely rebuilt over the summer of 1985; new facilities had been introduced with a sunshine roof, new toilet facilities, a large refreshment bar and an improved area for the disabled. The number of turnstiles was also increased from six to ten. The Merkland Stand, as it was now named, was formerly known as the Paddock. Originally, there had been plans to make the Merkland Stand a two-tier structure but costs, and reluctance from the local council to grant planning permission, scuppered the plans. There were also suggestions that there should have been a cantilever structure put in place, but lack of space for development and associated costs meant those plans were also shelved.

DARK BLUES TAKE THEIR BOW

Scotland defeated Wales 5-2 in the first-ever full international to be played at Pittodrie on February 3rd 1900. A record 12,000 crowd turned out generating receipts of £290. The local support turned out in force for what was the biggest football occasion to be held in the city. Hundreds of supporters made their way down King Street to the ground and special trams were commuting between the town centre and Pittodrie all day. Two goals in the opening seven minutes from John Bell of Celtic, and David Wilson of Queen's Park, set the Scots on their way to a comfortable victory.

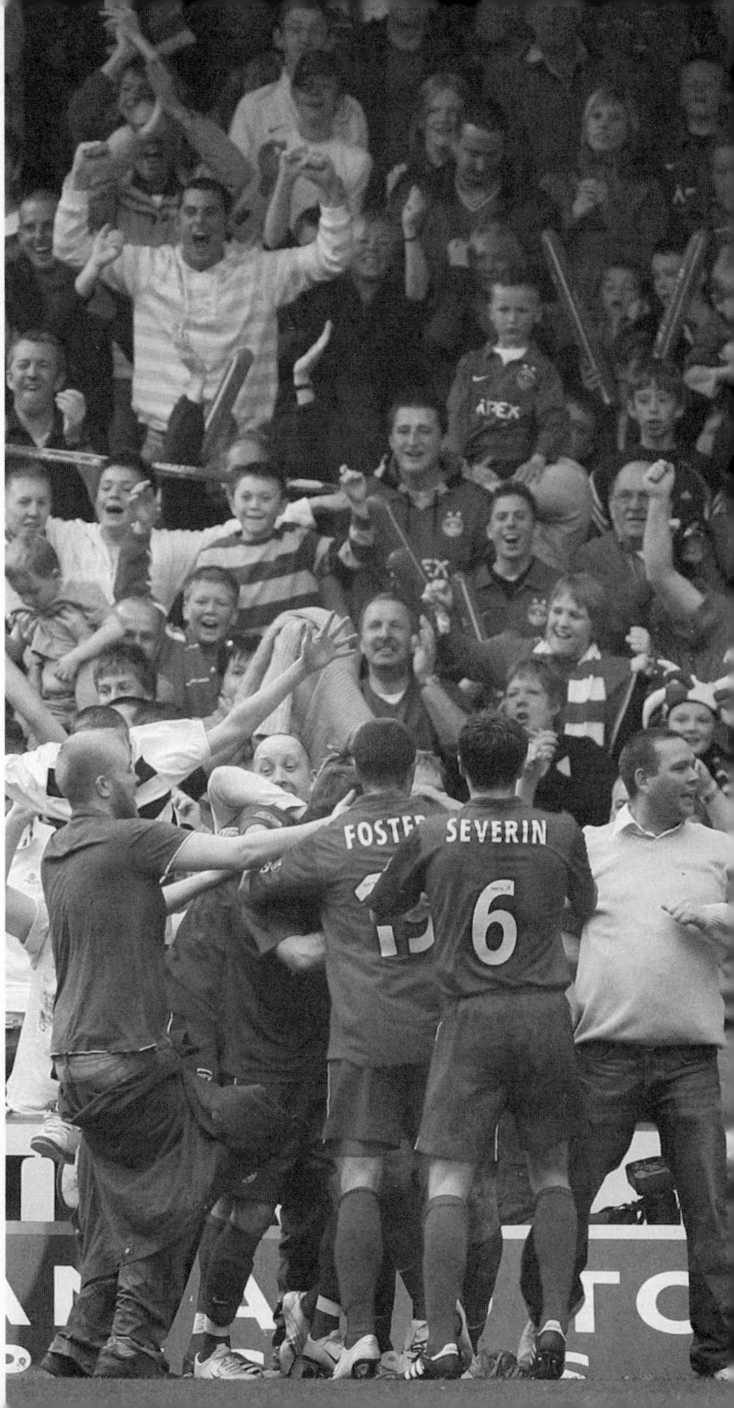

A TYPICAL CELEBRATION IN THE KING STREET END

SUPER DONS

As ECWC holders in 1983 Aberdeen became the only Scottish club to win two European titles when they beat old rivals SV Hamburg to win the European Super Cup. After a 0-0 draw in the Volkspark Stadion, the final was decided at a packed Pittodrie on December 20th 1983 when the Dons won 2-0 before an all-ticket capacity crowd; more than 80 countries took in the game live. Second-half goals from Neil Simpson and Mark McGhee fired Aberdeen into the history books.

GOODNIGHT VIENNA

Although Aberdeen should have been Scotland's first-ever European Cup representatives in 1955, it was not until 1980 that the Dons took their bow in the top European competition. After winning the Premier League the Dons went into the old format knockout tournament that preceded the Champions League. Aberdeen played their first-ever tie against Austrian champions Memphis at Pittodrie on 17th September 1980. Mark McGhee scored the only goal of the game and Aberdeen went through after a rearguard action in the Vienna return ended in a 0-0 stalemate.

WHAT'S IN A NAME?

Several theories have been put forward as to how the club came to be known as 'The Dons', the most popular being an abbreviation of Aberdonian. It was in a game in 1912 that the 'Dons' was heard for the first time. Previously, in 1881, when the original Aberdeen Football Club came into being, it was known that no less than eight teachers formed the original football club, which offers another theory to the nickname. The final theory was that the club was in close proximity to the River Don. When Aberdeen first played after the amalgamation in 1903, they were known as the 'Whites' for their first season by virtue of their new all-white strip. That only remained for the inaugural season. In 1904 the club entered the Scottish league and they changed to a black and gold striped shirt which hastened the new nickname of the 'Wasps' which was disliked by the players. That remained until the club changed to a red strip for the first time in March 1939.

CENTURIAN SCORERS

Eight Aberdeen players have managed to score 100 or more goals for the club in competitive matches. The table below does not include Drybrough Cup, Texaco Cup and associated cup competitions. Joe Harper remains the record club scorer, bagging 206 goals in his Aberdeen career in all competitions.

	Name	Date	Lge	LC	SC	Eur	Total
1	Joe Harper	1969-81	125	51	15	8	199
2	Matt Armstrong	1923-39	134	0	19	0	153
3	George Hamilton	1938-55	101	33	18	0	152
4	Harry Yorston	1947-57	98	22	21	0	141
5	Drew Jarvie	1972-82	85	29	7	10	131
6	Benny Yorston	1927-32	102	0	24	0	126
7	Willie Mills	1932-38	102	0	13	0	115
8	Jackie Hather	1948-60	78	16	10	0	104

DONS COME OF AGE

Hailed as the day the Dons came of age, it was a definitive moment in Aberdeen history when they defeated Rangers 4-1 in the 1982 Scottish Cup Final. Apart from laying a few Ibrox ghosts in the process, the victory opened the door to the European Cup Winners' Cup and, of course, Aberdeen went on to win in Europe the following season. For once Aberdeen went in to the Hampden final as firm favourites, given that the Rangers side was an ageing one; it was Aberdeen who were now on the threshold of a great spell. However, they had to prove their quality on the big stage and beating Rangers in their own backyard was vital. Much was made of Aberdeen freezing on the big stage just like they did in 1978; however, Alex Ferguson was having none of it. He knew exactly the quality he had at his disposal and despite Rangers taking the final to extra time, it was 'Fergie's Furies' who cut through Rangers in the additional period with three goals that resulted in such an emphatic win. It was future Rangers manager Alex McLeish who set Aberdeen on their way as his delightful curling shot from the edge of the box levelled the game. In extra time, goals from Mark McGhee, Gordon Strachan and a memorable goal from Neale Cooper consigned Rangers to a heavy defeat.

UP IN SMOKE

In the early hours of February 6th 1971 fire broke out in the Main Stand at Pittodrie which ripped through the club dressing rooms and administration areas. The result was devastating as many club records and artefacts were lost in the blaze. Fortunately, there were no injuries but the Dons' immediate form suffered as a consequence and the club continued to play their final home games after using a police meeting room as a makeshift dressing room. By the start of the following season the new offices and dressing rooms were built along with the 1,000 Main Stand seats that were destroyed in the fire.

WE SHALL NOT BE MOVED

Aberdeen share a record only matched by the Old Firm in Scotland in that they have never been relegated in their history. Since joining the Scottish League in 1904, the Dons' first season was in the old Second Division. After securing admission to the top division a year later, the club have remained there ever since. Despite the traumas that led to the club withdrawing from the league during the First World War, Aberdeen retained their status thereafter. The nearest Aberdeen came to being relegated was in 1995, and again in 2000. In 1995, it took an escape act that Houdini himself would have been proud of that culminated in a play-off win over Dunfermline Athletic. In 2000, the Dons finished bottom of the Premier League but were saved from the drop due to First Division winners Falkirk not having met the criteria set by the SPL. In the first season of the Premier League in 1975/76, the Dons just escaped going down after a 3-0 win on the last day against Hibernian at Pittodrie.

OUT OF AFRICA

Aberdeen have toured South Africa on three occasions in the past; in 1927, 1937 and 2006. In the 14 games played in 1927, Aberdeen won eight in what was a ground-breaking tour. Aberdeen also discovered scoring sensation Benny Yorston on the tour, which also brought in a £1,200 profit. Back then it took the Aberdeen party nearly three weeks to arrive in South Africa following a lengthy voyage by sea. Tragedy struck the Dons in 1937 when they lost winger Jackie Benyon who fell ill and died in Johannesburg of peritonitis.

COUNTRY OF ORIGIN EUROPEAN RECORD

Aberdeen have played German opposition more than any other country since the Dons made their European debut in September 1967. The Dons' 100th tie came against Hertha Berlin at Pittodrie in 2002. Aberdeen have never played teams from France and remain the only Scottish side that has won two European trophies with success in the European Cup Winners' Cup and European Super Cup in 1983. Aberdeen's record win came in their first-ever tie against Reykjavik of Iceland in a 10-0 first leg win at Pittodrie.

	P	W	D	L	F	A
Albania	2	1	1	0	1	0
Austria	4	2	1	1	3	2
Belgium	8	3	2	3	12	8
Bulgaria	4	2	1	1	7	3
Cyprus	2	2	0	0	5	0
Denmark	5	1	1	3	4	5
East Germany	4	1	1	2	3	5
England	6	1	2	3	6	12
Greece	1	0	0	1	0	3
Holland	2	1	0	1	2	2
Hungary	4	2	0	2	7	6
Iceland	8	7	1	0	31	5
Italy	4	0	1	3	4	8
Latvia	2	0	2	0	1	1
Lithuania	2	1	0	1	5	4
Moldova	2	1	1	0	1	0
Poland	4	2	1	1	3	1
Portugal	2	0	0	2	0	2
Rep of Ireland	6	4	1	1	10	4
Romania	2	1	1	0	5	2
Russia	1	0	1	0	1	1
Spain	6	4	0	2	7	7
Sweden	2	0	2	0	2	2
Switzerland	6	4	1	1	14	5
Ukraine	2	0	2	0	1	1
Wales	2	1	1	0	6	4
West Germany	16	4	5	7	20	29
Total	**109**	**45**	**29**	**35**	**161**	**122**

'SQUEAKY BUM TIME'

Perhaps more fashionably known as the 'business end' of the season, Aberdeen have been involved in many decisive moments in their history at this time of the year. In May 1995, the Dons were involved in a relegation battle that went down to the last seconds. In the penultimate game of the season, Aberdeen effectively consigned Dundee United to relegation after a narrow 2-1 win at Pittodrie. Aberdeen secured their status a week later with a win at Falkirk and a first-ever play-off success over Dunfermline Athletic. Four years earlier the final game of the 1990/91 season ended in bitter disappointment for the Dons as they went down 2-0 to Rangers at Ibrox. Needing a draw or a win to claim the championship, Aberdeen lost their nerve – and their 13-game unbeaten run – to hand Rangers the title. In 2008, Aberdeen defeated Rangers 2-0 in the final game of the season at Pittodrie. Had Rangers won and Celtic failed at Tannadice, the title would have gone to Ibrox.

NAP HAND DONS

Aberdeen have recorded many five-goal feats in their history. The most famous was the Dons' 5-0 win over Hibernian at Easter Road in May 1980. The convincing win helped Aberdeen clinch the Premier League title that day as Celtic failed to beat St Mirren. It was the Dons' first league success for 25 years and the first league success outside of Celtic and Rangers for 15 years. When Aberdeen went on to win the European Cup Winners' Cup in Gothenburg in 1983, their final game at Pittodrie was against Kilmarnock. The Dons warmed up for the final with a 5-0 win while their final game that season was also a 5-0 win over Hibernian on the last day as the players took their bow with the ECWC being paraded around the stadium. Aberdeen were also on the receiving end of a sensational 5-0 defeat to St. Johnstone in Perth in 1990. The Dons inexplicably collapsed against the Perth side and it was arguably the only blemish on a near faultless defensive record that season. Against Waterschei of Belgium in the 1983 ECWC semi-final, Aberdeen hit the little-known side in a 5-1 victory that set the Dons up for their first ever European final. The Dons' record Premier League win over Rangers was a 5-1 hammering at Pittodrie on January 19th 1985. Between 1969 and 1987, Aberdeen scored five or more goals in at least one league game for those 18 seasons.

NO CROWN FOR DONS

As part of the celebrations that were part of the Queen's Coronation to the throne in 1953, a British football tournament was held. The top four clubs from Scotland and England were invited to compete for the Coronation Cup, specially struck for the occasion. Aberdeen's involvement was brief as they came up against a strong Newcastle United side and went down 4-0 at Ibrox against the Geordies. Celtic went on to win the cup. The other competing sides were; Rangers, Hibernian, Manchester United, Tottenham and Arsenal.

ABERDEEN ANGUS

Angus the Bull has been the popular club mascot ever since he made his 'debut' at Pittodrie in August 1994. Derived from the famed Aberdeen Angus beef, the Dons mascot has thrilled Aberdeen supporters young and old for 15 years as part of the Pittodrie match-day experience.

CHRIS ANDERSON

Signed from Mugiemoss in 1944, Anderson went on to become a regular in the side in the early 1950s. After leaving Aberdeen and retiring from playing in 1956, Anderson returned to Pittodrie as a director on October 5th 1967 and went on to play a major part in the development of Aberdeen through the 1970s and the 1980s as Aberdeen conquered Europe. Chris Anderson was still on the Aberdeen board until his untimely death in May 1986.

PRIME MINISTER IN WAITING

Tony Blair may have gone on to become one of the most influential politicians of his generation, but Aberdeen played a big part in his efforts to become an MP as he set out as a young hopeful candidate in 1983. It was in his Sedgefield constituency, on the same night that Aberdeen were preparing to face Real Madrid in Sweden, that Blair was kept waiting and then invited to join his prospective committee as they gathered round to watch the Dons over a few beers. It was only when Aberdeen had won the cup that the respective members got round to putting Blair forward as a candidate for the Labour Party.

GREAT DANES

The Scandinavian invasion that was instigated by former Morton manager Hal Stewart in the 1960s saw Jens Petersén, Jorgen Ravn and Leif Mortensen join the Dons from the amateur leagues in Denmark in January 1965. Only Petersen, who was an established Danish international, would enjoy a prolonged spell with the club and the left-half went on to captain Aberdeen in 1969 before the emergence of Martin Buchan. Petersen played for Aberdeen in the 1967 Scottish Cup final before Henning Boel joined the club a year later. Boel went on to become a cult figure at Pittodrie with his trademark surging runs from his right-back position. Boel went on to win a Scottish Cup medal in 1970. The big defender left Aberdeen in 1973 after never fully recovering from a bad knee injury while playing against Borussia Monchengladbach in a Uefa Cup tie in Germany. Boel was spotted by the Dons while they were on tour to the USA in 1967. In 1999 Aberdeen appointed their first foreign manager when Ebbe Skovdahl arrived from Danish club Brondby. Skovdahl had been in charge of the Danish club that knocked Aberdeen out of the 1997 Uefa Cup. One of Ebbe's signings was international keeper Peter Kjaer who played for the Dons for nearly two years before announcing his retirement. Skovdahl's tenure at Pittodrie was largely uneventful with the club no further on when he left in 2002.

PULLING YOUR TEETH OUT

Two former Aberdeen players were also well known dentists. Sandy Grosert was part of the formidable Aberdeen side of the early 1920s and was believed to have been the earliest known dentist in Scottish football. He was born in Leith and played for Hibernian in the 1914 Scottish Cup final while studying as a dental student. Grosert was a hero during the war and was awarded the Military Cross after being wounded in action. He returned to Pittodrie in 1920 and received a benefit match that year. Tony Harris was born in Glasgow in 1923 before starting out with Queen's Park. He joined Aberdeen in 1946 and remained at Pittodrie for eight seasons. During his time at the club he was also a practising dentist in the city. Harris was also part of an attempted takeover of the club in 1969.

CHAMPIONS!

Aberdeen first became Scottish champions in 1955 when they won the old Division 'A' title under manager Dave Halliday. The Dons clinched their first title at Shawfield in a 1-0 win over Clyde, an Archie Glen penalty proving decisive. Aberdeen knew that a win at Shawfield would mean nearest challengers Celtic could not catch them. With the Dons due to visit Celtic Park the following week, the pressure was on Aberdeen, who had led from the front topping the league after the opening game and it was a position they were to hold for the season. In 1980 Aberdeen won the Premier League after clawing back a 12-point gap from one-time leaders Celtic. The bad winter of 1980, and the Dons' cup commitments, had meant that Aberdeen were behind in their league fixtures. Aberdeen had to defeat the Parkhead side twice in Glasgow in the league in April to help them to the championship that was clinched after a 5-0 win over Hibernian at Easter Road in May. With Celtic being held by third-placed St Mirren, the title celebrations began when manager Alex Ferguson ran on to the park and embraced Dons' veteran keeper Bobby Clark. It was in Edinburgh again in 1984 when Aberdeen won the title once more. On that occasion, a rare Stewart McKimmie goal gave the Dons a 1-0 win over Hearts at Tynecastle. Aberdeen retained the title for the first time a year later after a 1-1 draw against Celtic at Pittodrie gave Aberdeen an unassailable lead over their great rivals. Aberdeen's goal that day was scored by captain Willie Miller and the Dons wrapped up the title with three games left and also a record points haul. It was also the first time that Aberdeen clinched the league championship at Pittodrie. Ironically, on each of the four occasions that Aberdeen have won the championship, Celtic have been runners-up each time.

EUROPEAN TEAM OF THE YEAR

The title that was bestowed on Aberdeen after a sensational year in 1983 that brought two European successes to Pittodrie. After winning the European Cup Winners' Cup against Real Madrid in May, the Dons went on to claim the European Super Cup in December after beating European Cup holders SV Hamburg 2-0 at Pittodrie following a 0-0 draw in Germany. The much respected *France Football* declared Aberdeen as European Team of the Year to complete a memorable period for the club. Aberdeen remain, to this day, the only Scottish club that has won two European trophies.

DUTCH DELIGHT

It was former Aberdeen manager Alex Smith who was instrumental in tapping into the lucrative Dutch market for new signings. Smith took the view that most Scottish clubs were reluctant to sell their prized assets to rival clubs, so he turned to Holland in 1988 not long after taking over as Aberdeen manager. Smith's first signing was Theo Snelders who came in to replace Jim Leighton as the Dons' number one keeper. Snelders went on to enjoy cult status at the club until his departure in 1996. Aberdeen paid FC Twente £200,000 for his services. Other Dutch players followed such as Theo Ten Caat, Peter van de Ven, the towering Willem van der Ark and a club-record signing Hans Gillhaus. Aberdeen paid PSV Eindhoven £650,000 for the Holland international who was also a European Champions Cup winner with PSV. Gillhaus made an immediate impression with two goals on his debut at Dunfermline Athletic. One player who was also taken from the Dutch League was Paul Mason who was born in Liverpool but went on to become a popular player at Aberdeen after joining the Dons from Groningen in a £200,000 deal in 1988. Mason was actually part of the British exodus that worked in Holland in the 1980s and was employed as a bricklayer as well as playing for Groningen. Mason eventually left Aberdeen in 1993 and joined Ipswich Town in a £440,000 transfer.

THE 'KING'

Not an honour bestowed easily by an adoring Aberdeen support, but Joe Harper was the 'King' in their eyes. Harper joined Aberdeen in October 1969 in a record £40,000 deal from Morton. It was the beginning of two spells at Pittodrie that brought Harper iconic status with Aberdeen as an all-time record scorer for the club. Harper was part of the 1970 Scottish Cup side that defeated Celtic 3-1 at Hampden. Harper opened the scoring from the penalty spot. After being transferred to Everton in December 1972 for a record £172,000 deal, there was widespread anarchy on the terraces. After spells with Everton and Hibernian, Joe came 'home' in April 1976 in a £50,000 transfer from Hibernian. Several months later Harper was in the Aberdeen side that won the League Cup for the first time since 1955, and before his eventual retirement, he picked up a championship medal in 1980.

HONOURS

Aberdeen Football Club Honours: European Cup Winners' Cup Winners 1983; European Super Cup Winners 1983; Scottish League Champions 1955; Scottish Premier League Champions 1980, 1984, 1985; Scottish Cup Winners 1947, 1970, 1982, 1983, 1984, 1986, 1990; Scottish League Cup Winners 1955/56, 1976/77, 1985/86, 1989/90, 1995/96; Scottish Southern League Cup Winners 1945/46; Drybrough Cup Winners 1971, 1980; Scottish Qualifying Cup Winners 1904/05; Mitchell Cup Winners 1941/42, 1942/43, 1944/45; North Eastern League Winners 1941/42, 1942/43, 1943/44, 1944/45; Northern League Winners 1905/06, 1910/11; North Eastern Supplementary Cup Winners 1941/42, 1942/43; Highland League Championship Winners 1912/13, 1924/25; Aberdeenshire Cup Winners 1887/88, 1888/89, 1889/90, 1897/98, 1901/02, 1903/04, 1904/05, 1906/07, 1907/08, 1908/09, 1909/10, 1911/12, 1912/13, 1913/14, 1914/15, 1919/20, 1921/22, 1922/23, 1923/24, 1924/25, 1925/26, 1926/27, 1927/28, 1928/29, 1929/30, 1930/31, 1931/32, 1932/33, 1933/34, 1980/81, 1981/82, 1982/83, 1987/88, 1989/90, 1990/91, 1992/93, 1997/98, 2003/04, 2004/05; Aberdeenshire Charity Cup Winners 1891/92, 1897/98; Dewar Shield Winners 1906/07, 1908/09, 1912/13, 1914/15, 1926/27, 1928/29, 1930/31, 1931/32, 1932/33, 1933/34, 1935/36, 1936/37, 1939/40, 1945/46, 1949/50; Scottish Youth Cup Winners 1985, 1986, 2001; Scottish Premier Reserve League Champions 1981/82, 1986/87; Scottish Reserve League Champions 1955/56, 1972/73, 1981/82; Scottish Alliance League Champions 1932/33, 1935/36; Scottish Reserve League East Champions 1983/84; Scottish Second XI Cup Winners 1954/55, 1955/56, 1968/69, 1975/76, 1977/78, 1981/82; Scottish Reserve League Cup Winners 1956/57, 1957/58, 1972/73, 1978/79, 1979/80, 1984/85, 1996/97; Scottish League 'C' Division Champions 1952/53, 1954/55.

TURNBULL'S TORNADOES

Under manager Eddie Turnbull, the Dons gained a reputation for being a slick, stylish side as the club changed to a complete all-red strip. Known as the 'Turnbull Tornadoes', Aberdeen reached the 1967 Scottish Cup final only to lose to a Celtic side, creating their own piece of history. After three years in charge, Turnbull had transformed an ailing Aberdeen side into a free-scoring combine that was one of the top scoring sides in British football.

FIRST LEAGUE CUP FOR DONS

While Aberdeen had won very little by way of trophies before the war in 1939, that all changed in the immediate post war era. During the war years Aberdeen did well in the hastily arranged regional leagues and cup competitions. While the Dons side at that time were perhaps never fully tested by some weakened opposition, it gave the club a taste of success, something that had eluded them for many years. The Scottish League brought back football on a national level in 1945 and although the 1945/46 season was classified as unofficial, it gave the clubs and the supporters the chance to see competitive football once more. The Southern League Cup was brought into being for that season, which paved the way for the League Cup we know today. Aberdeen had fared well in the league coming third behind Rangers and Hibernian. In the cup, the Dons had battled their way past Kilmarnock, Hibernian, Partick Thistle, Ayr United and Airdrie to reach the Hampden final against Rangers. This was certainly new territory for the Dons but they stunned the huge 135,000 crowd by taking the lead in the first minute. Andy Cowie's long throw was flicked on by Stan Williams and Archie Baird ghosted in to head past Rangers keeper Shaw. It set the tone for an inspired opening spell for the Dons and they went further ahead in 18 minutes. Good work by George Hamilton and Alec Kiddie set up Stan Williams who unleashed an unstoppable shot past Shaw to put the Dons 2-0 ahead. Rangers came back strongly and eventually levelled the tie with 20 minutes left. Aberdeen finished the job in the last minute. Kiddie broke down the right and his cross was met by George Taylor who scored to give the Dons a sensational victory. There was no way back for Rangers and the joyous scenes after the game were mirrored in the north as the Aberdeen support gathered in their thousands at the Joint Station to welcome home their heroes. As luck would have it, the club were not trophy holders for very long. The league informed Aberdeen that their trophy would have to be returned as they were putting it forward as the Victory Cup; another hastily arranged competition that emerged on the back of the euphoria that surrounded the country following the end of the war. The Aberdeen team that day was; Johnstone, Cooper, McKenna, Cowie, Dunlop, Taylor, Kiddie, Hamilton, Williams, Baird, McCall.

ALLISTER, YOUNG AND GLEN

The heralded half-back line that helped Aberdeen to claim their first league title in 1955, Jackie Allister was a signing from Chelsea in 1952 and was the ball winner of the trio. Alex Young was the centre-half who was famed for his sliding tackles and his ability to outjump the tallest of opponents. Archie Glen provided the class as a left-half of great distinction who went on to play for Scotland. It was after the Dons won the Scottish championship that the half-back line was recognised as the best ever to wear the red of Aberdeen.

FIRST TIME OUT

The original Aberdeen Football Club played their first-ever game against Coupar Angus on March 11th 1882. After applying for Scottish Football Association membership on February 14th, the new club travelled south for the game and ended up losing 4-0. It was reported that each of the players paid their own fare on the train. The Aberdeen team that day was; Miller, A. V. Lothian, Hyslop, McHardy, Burns, Ross, Steele, Thomson, Stewart, D. B. Lothian and Glennie. Ten of the Aberdeen side were teachers. The first game in Aberdeen came on April 15th 1882 when Coupar Angus returned the favour and made the trip north. Aberdeen held a first club supper at the Queens Restaurant on the Friday evening before the game and after a first-ever team photograph the team went down 3-1 to their Tayside visitors at the Holburn cricket ground. The Aberdeen side contained eight teachers, one dentist, one bookbinder and one tailor. The visitors were welcomed at the Waverly Hotel after the game for tea and each member of the Aberdeen side paid 3s. 4d. – about 16p in new money. The club membership back then was given as 22 with J. Rose being the first-ever president of the club. A. V. Lothian was captain.

COUPAR ANGUS

Hardly a hotbed of football, but the Tayside club were the first-ever Aberdeen opponents on March 11th 1882. Aberdeen players paid their own fare as they travelled south before losing 4-0. Coupar Angus returned the favour a month later when they played in the first Association football game in Aberdeen. The game was played at the Holburn cricket ground and Aberdeen fared marginally better, going down 3-1.

AN UNQUALIFIED SUCCESS

The Scottish Qualifying Cup was the first national trophy won by Aberdeen after the amalgamation in 1903, and it is still competed for today by Highland League clubs as part of their Scottish Cup involvement. Aberdeen defeated Renton 2-0 at Dens Park in 1904 to lift the trophy. The success was seen as a major step forward in the club's efforts to gain admission to the top division. An estimated 1,500 supporters travelled down from Aberdeen for the final as a special British Caledonian train was laid on to take the supporters through to Dundee. On a frost bound pitch before a 10,000 crowd, Aberdeen players changed their footwear at the request of trainer Peter Simpson to take into account the slippery conditions. Several hundred supporters gathered outside the local press offices in Broad Street in Aberdeen as they awaited news from Dundee with regular updates being telegraphed through.

DAY THE DONS FROZE

It will be remembered as the day the Dons froze. Going down 2-1 to Rangers in the 1978 Scottish Cup final was a bitter blow for Aberdeen having gone undefeated in their previous 23 games. The fact that Aberdeen had defeated Rangers 4-0 and 3-0 in their last two matches made the final defeat all the more disappointing. When Aberdeen did eventually score it was without doubt the most bizarre goal ever seen at the national stadium. Steve Ritchie, a workmanlike left-back brought in from Hereford United that season for a £10,000 fee, was never renowned for scoring prowess. His effort in the closing minutes looked more like a mis-hit cross than anything else. However, even more strange were the attempts by Rangers keeper Peter McCloy to make a save. One can only assume that the giant Rangers keeper thought that Ritchie's effort was going over the bar, only for the ball to drop inside the goal to the absolute horror of McCloy.

SEEING DOUBLE

In May 1905, Aberdeen served up a double treat for their supporters with two matches that coincided with a Royal visit to the town that same day. First up was a fine 3-1 win by Aberdeen over Hearts in an East of Scotland League clash. Immediately after the game, the Aberdeen 'A' side romped to a 7-0 win over Bon Accord in a Fleming Shield cup tie.

CHAMPAGNE CHARLIE

Charlie Nicholas was the golden boy of Scottish football in the early 1980s with Celtic before his big move to London, and Arsenal, in 1983. Nicholas made as many headlines off the field as he did on it as the bright lights of the city proved attractive. In January 1988 it was Aberdeen manager Ian Porterfield who paid Arsenal £440,000 to take Charlie to Pittodrie. Such was his attraction that a crowd of 21,000 turned up for his first Pittodrie appearance for Aberdeen against Dunfermline Athletic. Nicholas went on to form a prolific partnership with Hans Gillhaus and regain his place in the Scotland squad before returning to his native Celtic in 1990 after he had helped the Dons win the Scottish Cup against his old team. After a spell with Clyde in the twilight of his career he became a well-known pundit with Sky Sports.

DENIS LAW: THE ONE THAT GOT AWAY

It remains one of the darkest moments in Aberdeen FC history that the greatest player ever to emerge from the city never got the chance to wear the red of his hometown club. When Alex Ferguson was manager at Pittodrie he proved to be a driving force for him to make sure that nothing like that would ever happen again. In fact, it was not until 1973 that Denis Law would grace Pittodrie for the first time when he captained Manchester City for the day as Aberdeen welcomed the English club to Pittodrie for a pre-season friendly on August 4th 1973. The Dons went on to lose the game 1-0, the first time an English club had succeeded at Pittodrie for 13 years. Law was given a standing ovation from the large Pittodrie crowd as he led his new Manchester City team on to the field.

HATHER THE HARE

Jackie Hather was the only English-born player in the Aberdeen side that won the league title in 1955. Dave Halliday spotted him playing for Annfield Plain and he persuaded Hather to turn professional with Aberdeen. Hather came from the Durham area and incredibly he defied medical opinion and played his entire career with one kidney. That did not prevent the Dons left winger from being the quickest player around, as he became known as the 'Hare'.

ABERDEEN IN THE LEAGUE CUP

Ever since winning the inaugural Southern League Cup in 1946, Aberdeen have gone on to win the League Cup on five occasions. After reaching the final in 1947, and the semi-final a year later, the Dons struggled for several years before their first official success in the tournament in 1955. Aberdeen were reigning league champions and were installed as favourites to beat St Mirren in the Hampden final. Aberdeen were the only undefeated team in Britain going into the game and eventually won through 2-1. Aberdeen showed a new found determination to succeed and added the League Cup to the championship title they won some months earlier. It was perhaps an indication of the Dons' rising stock in the game that they went in to the semi-final that year against Rangers as clear favourites... and they did not disappoint. In 1966 Aberdeen reached the semi-final under Eddie Turnbull only to go down to Rangers at Hampden in a replay. In 1976 Aberdeen took the trophy back to Pittodrie for the first time in 21 years. It took an extra-time goal from substitute Davie Robb to give Aberdeen victory after Drew Jarvie had levelled a Kenny Dalglish penalty. It was the first time that Willie Miller had led the Dons to success as he was to embark on a memorable career laden with silverware. In 1985, Alex Ferguson demanded his side win the one trophy that had eluded him in his memorable Pittodrie career and the Dons completed the task in some style by going through all six ties without conceding a single goal. Hibernian were no match for the Dons in the 12-minute final; noted after the Dons hit two goals in the opening period. The Dons' next success came in 1989, against Rangers, to win the tie in extra time. That win was crucial, as the Dons had lost the previous two finals to their arch rivals. In 1995 under Roy Aitken the Dons brought back a glimmer of the good old days by winning the cup against Dundee at Hampden. Goals from Dodds and Shearer took the cup north. Once again the Dons had to see the Old Firm off to succeed and that season it was Rangers and Paul Gascoigne who were put to the sword in the Hampden semi-final. It was a majestic performance from Eoin Jess that saw the Dons midfielder embarking on an extravagant piece of showboating in the closing minutes.

RANGERS UNDONE BY MASON

Described by Aberdeen captain Willie Miller as one of the most crucial successes in his Aberdeen career, the Dons won the League Cup against arch rivals Rangers in a pulsating final. This was the third League Cup final in succession that Aberdeen came up against Rangers; the Dons had lost the two previous meetings. The Aberdeen hero on the day was Liverpool-born Paul Mason whose two goals brought the League Cup back to Pittodrie in an act of defiance against the force of Graeme Souness and his array of highly paid international players. Mason put Aberdeen ahead in the 20th minute before a farcical penalty award allowed Walters to level before half-time. It was in the first period of extra time that Mason hit through a ruck of players to win the cup for Aberdeen. The Dons side that won the club's fourth League Cup was; Snelders, McKimmie, David Robertson, Grant, McLeish, Miller, Nicholas, Bett, Mason, Connor and Jess. Subs used; Brian Irvine, Willem van der Ark.

DOUGIE BELL

A surprise signing by Alex Ferguson in 1979, Bell was snapped up on a free transfer from St Mirren. Regarded by many as one of the most gifted and natural players at the club, Bell was perhaps not best suited for the rigours of the Scottish League. In the European arena it was an ideal platform for him; often used as a 'secret weapon' by Ferguson. It was Bell's tenacious running that opened the way for the Dons' comfortable win over Waterschei in the semi-final of the European Cup Winners' Cup at Pittodrie in April 1983. Bell was also outstanding against Bayern Munich in Germany but injury robbed him of a starting place against Madrid in the final. In 1986 he joined Rangers in a £130,000 transfer and also had spells with Hibernian, Shrewsbury Town and Birmingham City.

ARGES PITESTI

Aberdeen went through to the third round of a European competition for the first time after beating little-known Arges Pitesti in Romania. Earlier, the Dons had eclipsed holders Ipswich Town. Aberdeen had taken a 3-0 lead to Romania for the second leg and at one stage found themselves 2-0 down before a second-half comeback saw Aberdeen draw 2-2 to progress.

WHIPPING IT UP STATESIDE

In 1967 Aberdeen embarked on a tour of the USA that culminated in a sensational Presidents Cup final defeat to English side Wolverhampton Wanderers in a 6-5 'over time' finale. It completed an exhaustive tour as Aberdeen fought against the odds with a threadbare squad to reach the final as sides from all over the world took part. As part of the tournament, each club had to adopt an American name for the duration. Aberdeen ended up as the Washington Whips, a name that was chosen from 35,000 entries suggesting 5,400 names for the visiting Scots after a contest to decide the winning name. The criteria had to be symbolic of Washington, denoting aggression, action and excitement. Other names that were popular were the Washington Congressionals, Diplomats and Presidents. However, the most popular was the Whips and so Aberdeen, for six weeks in the summer of 1967, became the Washington Whips. One lucky winner who proposed the name earned themselves a two-week all-expenses-paid trip to Rome.

MILLER TIME

Several Millers have distinguished themselves for Aberdeen through the years. The best known was, of course, Aberdeen captain Willie Miller who led Aberdeen to glory in his 20 years with the club from 1971 to 1991. Namesake Johnny was the first Miller to make an impression at Pittodrie in the 1920s, joining Aberdeen from Liverpool, and went on to score 27 goals in 1921/22, his first season with the club. Bertie Miller signed for the club in 1971, in a £35,000 transfer from East Fife, and made 66 appearances for the club. Jimmy Miller was signed around about that time and Aberdeen had three Millers on their books in 1971 with Willie just joined from Eastercraigs. In 1984 a young Joe Miller made his debut and he went on to enjoy two spells for the club. The most recent Miller to make an impression is Lee Miller, who joined Aberdeen from Dundee United and went on to play for Scotland during his spell at Aberdeen.

WEE ALICKIE

The renowned original Aberdeen mascot was at all matches in the 1950s through to the 1970s and was famed in the local press as a cartoon figure with a one-liner on all Aberdeen games; a practice that remains to this day.

ABERDEEN OPPONENTS FOR FIRST TIME

Opponents	Date	H/A	Result	Competition
Airdrie	23.9.1905	A	0-2	Division 1
Albion Rovers	14.1.1905	A	0-1	Division 2
Alloa Athletic	23.1.1904	A	1-2	Scottish Cup
Arbroath	26.9.1903	H	1-2	Northern League
Ayr Utd	19.11.1904	A	3-3	Division 2
Berwick	25.1.1969	H	3-0	Scottish Cup
Brechin City	28.1.1911	H	3-0	Scottish Cup
Celtic	9.12.1905	A	0-1	Division 1
Clyde	27.8.1904	H	0-1	Division 2
Cowdenbeath	24.10.1903	A	1-3	Northern League
Dumbarton	8.2.1913	A	1-2	Scottish Cup
Dundee	18.11.1905	A	0-6	Division 1
Dundee United	14.11.1925	A	0-2	Division 1
Dunfermline	22.8.1903	H	2-4	Northern League
East Fife	5.2.1927	A	1-1	Scottish Cup
East Stirling	5.11.1904	A	4-1	Division 2
Elgin City	22.1.1938	A	6-1	Scottish Cup
Falkirk	20.8.1904	H	1-2	Division 2
Forfar Athletic	31.10.1903	H	3-1	Northern League
Gretna	29.9.2007	H	2-0	SPL
Hamilton	10.9.1904	H	3-3	Division 2
Hearts	28.10.1905	A	1-1	Division 1
Hibernian	16.9.1905	H	2-1	Division 1
Inverness CT	8.8.1998	A	3-0	League Cup
Kilmarnock	2.9.1905	H	2-0	Division 1
Livingston	23.1.1999	H	0-1	Scottish Cup
Montrose	14.11.1903	H	4-2	Northern League
Morton	4.11.1905	H	3-0	Division 1
Motherwell	13.1.1906	A	3-3	Division 1
Partick Thistle	19.8.1905	H	0-1	Division 1
Peterhead	10.2.1923	H	13-0	Scottish Cup
Queen of the South	21.10.1933	H	5-0	Division 1
Queen's Park	28.1.1905	H	2-1	Scottish Cup
Raith Rovers	22.10.1904	H	3-1	Division 2
Rangers	28.8.1905	A	0-1	Division 1

St Johnstone	29.8.1903	H	5-1	Northern League
St Mirren	30.9.1905	A	2-4	Division 1
Stenhousemuir	15.8.1903	H	1-1	Northern League
Stirling Albion	19.11.1949	A	1-0	Division 1
Stranraer	17.8.1994	H	1-0	League Cup

THE MOORE THE MERRIER

Paddy Moore was a prolific scorer for the club in his short spell at Aberdeen in 1932. The Irishman had the distinction of scoring six goals for the Dons against Falkirk on September 14th 1932. Moore's greatest feat, however, came for his country in a World Cup tie against Belgium in Dublin in 1934. Trailing 4-0 at one stage, Moore went on to score all four goals as the Irish went on to draw the game 4-4. Alex Merrie is the only other Dons player that has scored six goals in a competitive game. Merrie hit six against a hapless Hibernian side at Pittodrie in a 7-0 rout on November 15th 1930. Merrie only ever played 32 first-team games for Aberdeen, but scored an amazing 26 goals.

MONEY MADNESS

Craig Hignett will never go down in any loyalty scheme after an eventful spell at Pittodrie in 1998. Signed from Middlesbrough, the midfielder became the highest earner at the club on a reported £8,000 per week salary. The complete folly of the deal was exposed when it emerged some time later that Hignett also had a 'loyalty bonus' payment every three months as part of his deal. Aberdeen recouped some of that money when he was sold to Barnsley after only four months.

EXECUTIVE DECISION

On the back of the success Aberdeen achieved at home and in Europe in 1983, the club installed new 'executive' boxes at the rear of the Main Stand at Pittodrie. Spreading the entire length of the stand, they were built to accommodate the expanding corporate market. Following the completion of the Richard Donald Stand in 1993, there was a substantial increase to the corporate facilities within the new structure.

DONS NOT UNDER PAR

Aberdeen came up against Dunfermline Athletic in what was a first-ever Premier League play-off in 1995. After finishing second bottom in the league, Aberdeen had to play the First Division runners-up to see who would be playing in the top flight the following season. It was a double from Duncan Shearer that helped Aberdeen to an impressive, but nervous, 3-1 first-leg lead. Dunfermline arrived at Pittodrie protecting a 15-game unbeaten run but they were met with a frenzied Pittodrie atmosphere that lifted the Aberdeen players. The Dons set about their task and took full advantage of their visitors' nerves and eventually made the breakthrough in 38 minutes. Stephen Glass curled a precise free kick over the Dunfermline wall when everyone was expecting Duncan Shearer to be more direct. Pittodrie was stunned in 48 minutes when former Don Craig Robertson rose to head a Moore cross past Snelders. That heightened the tension but seven minutes later Duncan Shearer restored order when he stooped to head home a McKimmie lob. There was a decisive moment on 61 minutes when captain McKimmie seemed to be colliding with Moore in the box. Had the Dunfermline player not made so much out of the challenge, referee Mottram may well have given the penalty. As it was, the tie swung the Dons' way as they piled on the pressure; young Stephen Glass weaved his way past three defenders before just missing the target. With only three minutes left it was that man Shearer who scored again, taking a Brian Irvine through-ball on the run before volleying past Van de Kamp. It was all too much for Pars boss Bert Paton who was angry after the game; "We did not get many breaks and I am disappointed in not getting a penalty kick. Obviously, at 3-1 it is going to be tough but we still have a chance." Duncan Shearer was happy to give his team a vital cushion for the return leg; "I felt jaded at times, the pressure was unbelievable. The support was fantastic and I have never heard such noise from them. I could hardly hear anything on the field and I think Dunfermline were a bit nervous because of that." Aberdeen went on to win comfortably at East End Park in another 3-1 win before another amazing support. More than 8,000 Red Army followers made it, and their presence dampened the enthusiasm of the home side despite manager Paton trying to fire up his team.

GOLDEN GOALS

In the days of the famed black and gold, Aberdeen never managed to secure a first national trophy but it was not for the want of trying. In season 1932/33, the club scoring records were equalled with 85 league goals scored from 38 matches. That did not make that much difference in the final league table but Irish international Paddy Moore helped with three hat-tricks during that season with Willie Mills also scoring three in an 8-1 rout of Clyde.

DONS LUCKY 13 IN LEAGUE CUP

Thirteen Aberdeen players have scored for the club in League Cup finals: Graham Leggat 1955; Drew Jarvie and Dave Robb 1976; Duncan Davidson 1979; Eric Black (2) and Billy Stark 1985; Jim Bett, John Hewitt and Willie Falconer 1987; Davie Dodds (2) 1988; Paul Mason (2) 1989; Duncan Shearer 1992 and 1995; Billy Dodds 1995.

DAZZLING DEBUTS

Arguably the most stunning debut from an Aberdeen player was Hans Gillhaus' tremendous showing against Dunfermline Athletic in November 1989. The Dons record £650,000 buy from PSV Eindhoven scored two sensational goals in a 3-0 win. Another Don who scored twice on his debut was Duncan Shearer. The Highland hitman introduced himself to the Pittodrie faithful with a brace against Hibernian in August 1992. However, they would have to go some to beat the grandly named Augustus Lowe who scored all four Aberdeen goals on his debut against East Stirling on November 5th 1904 in the Dons' first season in league football.

REVENGE IS SWISS

FC Sion were the team the Dons met in their opening tie in the 1982/83 European Cup Winners' Cup competition. Aberdeen crushed the Swiss side 7-0 at Pittodrie before embarking on a glory run that ended in triumph in Gothenburg. Three years later the Swiss exacted revenge as they comfortably knocked Aberdeen out of the 1986 ECWC in what was Alex Ferguson's last game in charge of the Dons in European football. After a 2-2 home win, Aberdeen fell apart in Sion and crashed following a 3-0 second leg defeat.

'WHITES' TAKE THEIR BOW

The protracted negotiations that took place between the three clubs that formed Aberdeen FC in April 1903 were settled and the combined effort was to concentrate on the playing side. It was perhaps fortunate that Aberdeen had not been allowed admission into the league at the first time of asking; a probable relegation would almost certainly have followed and the club's proud 100-year record would never have evolved. As it was, the new Aberdeen Football Club had to cut their teeth in the Northern League, which had been set up in the early 1890s. There certainly was unprecedented interest in the first game at home to Stenhousemuir on August 15th 1903 as a crowd of 8,000 turned out at Pittodrie for the opening game. Aberdeen – in a new all white strip – won the toss and elected to defend the east goal. The crowd were certainly up for the occasion and as referee Hendry got the game under way there were loud cheers from those present. No doubt encouraged by the big crowd, the Aberdeen forwards look impressive in the opening spell. After 20 minutes the 'Whites' took the lead with a superb goal. Captain Willie MacAulay carved out an opening and hit a screamer past the Stenhousemuir keeper Wood to open the scoring. Despite taking the game to the visitors it was former Scotland international keeper Frank Barrett that helped protect the Aberdeen lead with a couple of marvellous saves; one in particular from Brown was truly international class. Aberdeen returned to the offensive in the second half in search of a second goal that would surely secure victory. Visiting keeper Wood was in fine form and despite Aberdeen taking the game to Stenhousemuir; it was the visitors who hit back with 20 minutes left. Aberdeen's David McKay went close with a shot that came back off the bar and as luck would have it Stenhousemuir levelled almost immediately. Sandy McNair's shot went in off the post with Barrett, for once, beaten. It may have been harsh on Aberdeen but the equaliser meant that the game reached a frantic closing spell with neither side able to take advantage. The game ended all square and it was interesting to note the contrast in styles; the more experienced Stenhousemuir adopted a passing game while the home side, no doubt encouraged by their newfound status, opted for a more direct approach. ABERDEEN: Barrett, Willox, McGregor, Sangster, Low, Ritchie, C. Mackie, Strang, McKay, MacAulay, Johnston.

POLES APART

On their way to the final of the European Cup Winners' Cup in 1983, the Dons came up against Polish side Lech Poznan in the second round. Poland, at that time, was a country in turmoil as the trade union uprisings in the industrial heartlands had caused huge political and social unrest. Travelling to the country, which was under Martial Law, was proving hazardous and for that reason alone manager Ferguson was adamant that his team take a good lead to Poznan for what was sure to be a daunting trip. In the first leg at Pittodrie on October 20th 1982 the Dons dominated the tie but only had goals from Peter Weir and Mark McGhee to show for their efforts. Two weeks later the Aberdeen party arrived in Poznan in Eastern Poland and were greeted with a covering of snow in freezing weather conditions. The imposing stadium in Poznan was being run by the military in a setting that more resembled a scene from the war film *Escape To Victory* than a European tie. However, Aberdeen did not have to rely on the extravagance of Sylvester Stallone to overcome a spirited and often frenzied Polish side. In front of a partisan 30,000 home crowd, the Dons mastered Poznan with a maturity that belied their European inexperience. The crowd was silenced when Doug Bell claimed the only goal of the game after 59 minutes.

SHAWFIELD GONE TO THE DOGS

The old home ground of Clyde, situated in Rutherglen, Glasgow was the scene of the Dons' first-ever title triumph in 1955. Shawfield was also better known for the dog racing that has been held there, and the track around the playing surface made for an eerie atmosphere. It took an Archie Glen penalty to clinch the title. Glen had shared the penalty-taking responsibilities with Jackie Allister and it was Glen who actually missed his previous kick some weeks earlier. With Allister not in the side, the responsibility fell on Glen once again, and he dispatched his kick high into the net. The game also saw the last first-team appearance for George Hamilton. The Aberdeen players had to wait until news of Hearts' defeat at Ibrox filtered through as they still had a mathematical chance of catching the Dons had they won handsomely against Rangers.

IRISH EYES ARE SMILING

It is a common belief that Willie Lennie was the Dons' first capped player for Scotland back in 1908. Although that is true, the first Aberdeen player to be capped for his country was Lennie's teammate Charlie O'Hagan. Born in Buncrana in 1882, it was when O'Hagan was with Tottenham that he produced the kind of form that was to lead to his first cap for Ireland against Scotland on March 18th 1905. It was following a brief spell with Middlesbrough in 1906, where he played in only six matches, that Aberdeen manager Jimmy Philip took an almost nomad-like O'Hagan to Pittodrie. On March 14th 1908, O'Hagan found himself in opposition to his great friend as Lennie was in the Scotland side and O'Hagan had the distinction of leading Ireland. It was Lennie who came through smiling as the Scots went nap in a 5-0 win at Dublin's Dalymount Park. Charlie O'Hagan eventually left Aberdeen and joined Greenock Morton in 1910. He made 112 appearances for the Dons, scoring 24 goals. Joe O'Reilly joined Aberdeen in 1932, from Irish side Brideville, in the immediate aftermath of the 'Great Mystery' that rocked Pittodrie to the core in November 1931. O'Reilly took his chance in the Aberdeen first team and played more than 40 matches for the Dons, as well as establishing himself in the Ireland side. O'Reilly went on win 20 international caps, the first of which came against the Netherlands in a 2-0 win in May 1932. After two years at Pittodrie, O'Reilly moved back to his native Brideville after failing to cement a right-half place in the Aberdeen side. The 1930s produced several Irish players in the Scottish League and among them was Paddy Moore, another Irish international. Moore will go down in club history, along with Alex Merrie, as being the only two Aberdeen players to score six goals for the club in a single game. Born in Ballybough in 1909, Paddy became another player to play for both Eire and Northern Ireland when he was selected to play against England. After his transfer to Aberdeen he created his own piece of history when he scored all four Ireland goals in a 4-4 draw against Belgium in a World Cup tie. In his three seasons at Pittodrie, Moore notched an impressive 47 goals from only 74 appearances before he returned to his beloved Shamrock in July 1935. Before returning to Shamrock for a fourth time, Paddy Moore had spells with Shelbourne and Brideville. Paddy Moore died aged 42 in July 1951.

DRYBROUGH CUP 1980

It is not very often that a captain will have the honour of lifting two trophies in consecutive days, but Dons skipper Willie Miller was getting into the habit of making sure the successful times continued in 1980. After Aberdeen had made a significant breakthrough by winning the league championship that year, expectations were high that the club would be able to sustain a challenge in all competitions. Manager Alex Ferguson was convinced that his side was on the verge of something special as he was sure that the league win would prove a vital factor. "We have taken a huge step forward by winning the title. The players have shown that they can not only match but overcome the Old Firm in the long haul and that will be crucial for sustained success in the future." At the beginning of the 1980/81 season, the Dons warmed up for the new campaign with victory in the last-ever Drybrough Cup match and 24 hours later they welcomed Arsenal to Pittodrie where they were officially presented with the league championship trophy and the unfurling of the league flag. The Dons had progressed to their second Drybrough Cup final after a home win over Airdrie and three days later a hard fought 4-2 victory over Morton at Cappielow. The Drybrough Cup proved very popular when it first emerged in 1971 when the Dons beat Celtic in the Pittodrie final. Ten years on the pre-season tournament had ran its course and the Aberdeen v St Mirren final at Hampden was the last ever Drybrough Cup match.

WATERSCHEI

This little-known team from Belgium was defeated by Aberdeen in their 1983 European Cup Winners' Cup semi-final. With Austria Vienna and Real Madrid making up the other qualifiers, Aberdeen boss Alex Ferguson made no secret of the fact that he wanted the Belgians in the draw. Aberdeen did come up against the side that had knocked out one of the tournament favourites, Paris St. Germain, in the quarter-final. In a whirlwind start at Pittodrie the Dons swept the Belgians aside and raced into a 2-0 lead. The eventual 5-1 win did not flatter Aberdeen who completed the job in Genk in the return leg; although losing the game 1-0, the Dons eased through to a first-ever European final.

HICHAM ZEROUALI 1977-2004

The unknown Hicham Zerouali certainly had the Aberdeen fans on the edge of their seats after he joined the Dons in November 1999 from Moroccan club Fus Rabat. Sadly, Hicham met his untimely death after a road accident in his native Morocco in December 2004. 'Zero' as he was affectionately known by the Aberdeen support, scored three goals for his country and also played in the African Nations Cup finals in Mali in 2002. Hicham Zerouali was born in Morocco on January 17th 1977 and began his career with Yaakoub El Mansour before joining Police Union and then Fus Rabat. It was while he was at Rabat that he attracted the attention of Aberdeen, which prompted his £450,000 transfer. Zerouali arrived at Aberdeen when the Dons were struggling at the foot of the SPL and he made his debut against Hearts at Pittodrie on December 8th 1999. Coming on as a second-half substitute, the magical Moroccan gave the Aberdeen support a taste of what was to come with some wonderful touches and superb close control. His impact was immediate as Aberdeen went on to win the game 3-1 with Hicham setting up two of the Aberdeen goals. Zerouali went on to make 20 appearances for the Dons that season, scoring five goals, which helped Aberdeen to reach both domestic cup finals that season. Among those goals was a spectacular strike against St Mirren in Paisley. That helped Aberdeen to take the tie back to Pittodrie and it was a milestone in the Dons history as it was the club's 700th goal in the Scottish Cup. Zerouali's sublime skills had earned him a call-up to the Moroccan national side but his Aberdeen career was cut short following a dreadful injury sustained after a clash with Motherwell's Ged Brannan at Fir Park on August 27th 2000. The ankle break curtailed his appearances that season and it was suggested that he was never the same player after he finally returned to action nearly a year later. Hicham was so popular with the Aberdeen support that many fans sported fezzes during his early Pittodrie days; his trademark somersaults after scoring brought him cult status with the Red Army.

	Lge	SC	LC	Euro	Total	Goals
1999/00	14	4	2	0	20	5
2000/01	5	0	0	2	7	0
2001/02	18	1	2	0	21	8
Total	37	5	4	2	48	13

TEDDY SCOTT

Teddy Scott: the most loyal servant to Aberdeen Football Club was cast in various roles; player, coach, trainer and kit man. For someone who has served under 16 different managers at the club, he has seen and done it all. Teddy first came to prominence as a young centre-half for Aberdeen junior club Sunnybank. Previously, he had been playing his schools football at Ellon Secondary. His career continued with Caley Thistle under-18s before he moved to Sunnybank. The Heathryfold club were blazing a trail in tandem with the Dons in 1954. While Aberdeen were making their way to the Scottish Cup final at Hampden, Sunnybank were creating their own piece of history by going all the way in the Junior Cup, defeating Lochee Harp 2-1 in the final. Teddy signed for Aberdeen on March 3rd 1954 and made his first appearance in the red shirt of Aberdeen in the public trial match at Pittodrie on August 6th 1954. Regular centre-half Alec Young was regarded as the best in the country while Jim Clunie was emerging from the reserve side. Against this fierce competition, Teddy's playing career never really got out of the starting blocks. Although Teddy was only 5ft 7ins. tall he made up for his lack of height with a leaping ability that was likened to Eddie Falloon from the famous Aberdeen side of the 1930s. In those days the typical centre-half was a tall commanding figure, but that was soon to change. The record books reveal that Teddy only ever played once for the first team; a 2-0 win at Stirling Albion on February 25th 1956. It was during the latter part of the 1956/57 season that Teddy was loaned to Brechin City and following a free transfer from the club he moved to Elgin City in the Highland League. After one season at Borough Briggs, Teddy returned to Pittodrie to take up a training role under manager Dave Shaw. The situation altered somewhat when Tommy Pearson took over as manager and Shaw reverted to his previous trainer's position. For many years Teddy coached and nurtured the young Dons players always keen to offer a word in their ear. The testimonies that came flooding in after he announced his retirement in 2004 gave some indication just how much value they had placed on his contribution. Alex Ferguson remains one of his close friends and the Manchester United manager could not have paid Teddy Scott a higher tribute by taking his full side up to play Aberdeen in Teddy's testimonial in January 1999.

THE IRON MAN

Loyalty is such a rare commodity in the modern game. Back in the 1960s such loyalty was epitomised by players who spent almost their entire career with one club. Ally Shewan certainly came into that category. Ally joined the Dons in 1960 from Formartine United and after a short spell in the reserve team he made his debut against Dundee at Dens Park in January 1962. Shewan proved to be a model of consistency by creating a club record when he made 162 consecutive league appearances between 1963 and 1969. Ally developed in to a tough character, epitomised by the title bestowed upon him by the American public in 1967; 'The Iron Man' as he was known when the Dons toured the States in 1967. Ally's open feuds and running battles with Wolves' Derek Dougan in the memorable clashes with the English club in America perhaps epitomised what football meant to Ally, his never-say-die attitude dragged Aberdeen through many a struggle. Shewan was in the Aberdeen side that played Celtic in the 1967 Scottish Cup Final and he eventually left the Dons in 1969 after a disagreement with terms. Ally decided to join the exodus to Australia where he joined Sydney club Budapest but his stay there was a short one – little more than a week. Ally returned to his native north-east and served Elgin City in the Highland League for many years. Ally returned to Pittodrie with his Elgin side to take on Scottish Cup holders Aberdeen in 1971 in what was his final appearance at his beloved Pittodrie. In his nine seasons at the stadium, Ally Shewan made 301 appearances, scoring nine goals.

PIONEERING SPIRIT

The club embarked on their first foreign tour on May 10th 1911 when they journeyed to Bohemia and Poland. The journey took the best part of four days and Aberdeen were the first Scottish club to tour Eastern Europe. The Aberdeen party was met with widespread curiosity as well as a friendly welcome. Aberdeen had barely got off their train after the exhaustive journey when they suffered their only defeat; a 3-2 loss to Slavia Prague. Such was the Scots' popularity that they actually played two games on 23rd May; against Prerau (8-0) and Brunn (6-1). The Brunn game was an unscheduled one as the local team insisted the Aberdeen side played them when their train stopped en route to Poland.

FIRST SCOTTISH CUP TIE

The Scottish Cup has provided generations of Aberdeen followers with some great highs and lows throughout the years, and the club has built up a tradition in the national competition on the back of an outstanding record. The cup itself can be traced back to 1873, when the inaugural competition was won by Queen's Park. The success was a culmination of a year's effort when, at a meeting of eight clubs in Glasgow's Bridge Street in March of that year, the Scottish Cup became a reality. At that meeting, the Scottish Football Association was formed and 15 clubs contributed to the cost of making the trophy and a set of medals. The total cost amounted to 56 pounds, 12 shillings and 11d. Aberdeen's first venture into the national competition was to come in 1882, some nine years after the first Scottish Cup competition. The news was met with no little apprehension in the north, as no one really knew anything about the cup, which had been the sole property of the established clubs in the central belt. In the first round of the 1882/83 competition, Aberdeen were drawn at home against Dundee Harp. It is not clear if this draw was done on a regional basis. As there is no record of Dundee Harp in the later rounds it was assumed that the Aberdeen tie was indeed a first round clash. Aberdeen managed to secure use of the Grammar grounds as they were the only school that had an enclosed pitch in the area at that time. On October 7th 1882, Harp came north to play Aberdeen in their first-ever Scottish Cup tie. Aberdeen: J. Jamieson, A. Lothian, R. Hyslop, C. Glennie, J. McHardy, C. Wilson, A. Steele, D. Smith, W. Stewart, A. Ross, D. Lothian. Dundee Harp: McTaggart, Clarke, Denny, O'Leary, Holmes, Shields, Elloy, McMahon, Rock, Castro, Sutton. The visitors almost took the lead in the first minute, but the referee ruled out Harp's effort. In a hard fought contest, the visitors' pressure eventually proved fruitful when they took the lead just before half-time. Aberdeen continued to take the game to the Dundee side, and they were rewarded when a superb solo run from winger Lothian ended with the Aberdeen man scoring the club's first-ever goal in the national competition. Harp retaliated and were fortunate to take the lead again after scoring from a disputed free kick. A minute from time, the visitors scored again to end any fading hopes of an Aberdeen fightback. Result: Aberdeen 1, Dundee Harp 3. Attendance: 400.

DONS SMASH THE 'IRON CURTAIN'

Aberdeen went into their Scottish Cup semi-final against Rangers at Hampden on April 10th 1954 as outsiders, but the final outcome was a staggering 6-0 win for Aberdeen in what was their first-ever Scottish Cup victory over their great rivals. The Rangers defence had become known as the 'Iron Curtain' due to their miserly approach and physical strength. The Dons swept the 'Gers aside in what remains the Ibrox club's worst defeat in Scottish Cup history. Hero of the day was Aberdeen inside-forward Joe O'Neil – shunned by the Ibrox club as a youngster – who helped himself to a memorable hat-trick in the rout before a 111,000 crowd. What was all the more remarkable was the fact that O'Neil had suffered from a fractured skull in a match against Falkirk only three weeks previously. Against medical advice and declaring to Aberdeen boss Dave Halliday that he was fit, Joe played against Rangers as further goals from Graham Leggat, Jackie Allister and Paddy Buckley made it a joyous day for Aberdeen and their sizeable support at the national stadium.

DOUBLE SHUFFLE

Former Aberdeen player and manager Tommy Pearson developed the double-shuffle technique during wartime football; a move that added trickery to the winger's array of skills. Pearson had the distinction of playing for both Scotland and England in international football; his appearance for the English came as a last minute replacement in a wartime international. Pearson started out with Newcastle United in 1933 where he remained until after the war. Pearson joined Aberdeen in a £4,000 deal in 1948 and at 35 years of age he was in the twilight of his career. Such was his popularity as a player of genuine skill, several thousand would regularly turn up for Aberdeen reserve matches to see Pearson in action. After retiring from playing in 1953, Tommy turned his hand to journalism with the *Daily Mail*. After being appointed youth coach at Pittodrie in 1959, he took over as manager in November that year. Pearson turned to youth at Pittodrie as the Dons sold several of their more experienced players. Several poor results in the Scottish Cup ultimately led to his downfall. It was in 1965, in the aftermath of the Dons' Scottish Cup defeat to lowly East Fife, that Tommy Pearson resigned as Aberdeen boss.

ALLY'S ARMY

"We're on the march with Ally's Army" was the excruciating blast that went down on vinyl in 1978 as Scotland went to Argentina for the World Cup finals. Leading the squad was Ally MacLeod, the manager who was brought in to lead the Scots after a successful spell in charge of Aberdeen. While Scotland had promised to do the country proud, they ended up coming home early, and in disgrace, as a disastrous tournament on and off the field came to a close. MacLeod had seemed out of his depth; a far cry from his 18-month spell at Pittodrie. Ally came in to replace Jim Bonthrone in November 1975 and immediately whipped up a new enthusiasm and promised the support a trophy within twelve months. Ally duly delivered with a League Cup win over Celtic in 1976.

LEAGUE CUP CLEAN SHEET

The one trophy that had eluded Alex Ferguson in his spell in charge of Aberdeen was the League Cup. In 1985 the Dons set the record straight by lifting the trophy in impressive fashion as they did not lose a single goal in all six ties. After beating Ayr United 5-0 and St. Johnstone 2-0 in the early rounds, Hearts were defeated 1-0 at Pittodrie while Dundee United could not find a way through in both legs of the semi-final. Hibernian reached the Hampden final but were swept aside in a 3-0 win. Jim Leighton played in all six ties.

THE EIGHT-MINUTE PENALTY

It would not happen these days but when Aberdeen were awarded a penalty in the 1970 Scottish Cup final, it took an astonishing eight minutes before Joe Harper could finally take the kick. Derek McKay's cross was handled by Bobby Murdoch and referee Bob Davidson awarded Aberdeen the spot kick. Such were the protests from the Celtic players, and the usual round of cautions, some of the Celtic player then continued incredible gamesmanship by knocking the ball off the spot and trying to put Harper off with verbal taunts and continued delays. When wee Joe finally was allowed to take the kick, he duly gave Evan Williams no chance to put Aberdeen ahead. Harper was the epitome of cool as he turned to celebrate with the massed ranks of Aberdeen supporters in the Mount Florida end of the ground.

BADGE OF HONOUR

Alex Ferguson once said that it was a "sin" that managers were not awarded winners' medals like the players during the Dons' successful period under him. The managers' table reflects Ferguson way ahead of any other Aberdeen manager in the club's history with ten major titles during his seven-year spell with the club. Only six other Aberdeen managers have tasted success during the Dons' 106-year history. Dave Halliday was the first to bring silverware to Pittodrie after the war in 1945 and the only other manager, apart from Ferguson, to win all three domestic trophies. The nearest to that came with the Alex Smith/Jocky Scott co-manager partnership that almost completed a full set in 1991 when they just failed to take the title to Pittodrie.

Name	LC	SC	Lge	Eur	Total
Aitken, Roy	1	0	0	0	1
Bonthrone, Jim	0	0	0	0	0
Calderwood, Jimmy	0	0	0	0	0
Ferguson, Alex	1	4	3	2	10
Halliday, Dave	1	1	1	0	3
Hegarty, Paul	0	0	0	0	0
MacLeod, Ally	1	0	0	0	1
McNeill, Billy	0	0	0	0	0
Miller, Alex	0	0	0	0	0
Miller, Willie	0	0	0	0	0
Paterson, Steve	0	0	0	0	0
Pearson, Tommy	0	0	0	0	0
Philip, Jimmy	0	0	0	0	0
Porterfield, Ian	0	0	0	0	0
Shaw, Dave	1	0	0	0	1
Skovdahl, Ebbe	0	0	0	0	0
Smith, Alex/Scott, Jocky	1	1	0	0	2
Travers, Pat	0	0	0	0	0
Turnbull, Eddie	0	1	0	0	1
Totals	**6**	**7**	**4**	**2**	**19**

Above table includes 1946 Southern League Cup win, officially recognised at that time.

MR CHAIRMAN

One name will be synonymous with Aberdeen Football Club and that is Dick Donald. Dick served the club he loved as a player, director and chairman with a pride and distinction that few could imagine. While Dick would find it difficult to be remembered as a player of great ability, his work behind the scenes ensured that Aberdeen, as a club, fulfilled ambitions beyond all expectations which culminated in 1983 when Aberdeen conquered Europe. Along with Chris Anderson and Charles Forbes, Dick Donald steered Aberdeen to the top at both home and abroad. Dick enjoyed five seasons at Pittodrie as a player before joining Dunfermline Athletic, but he was soon to return to Aberdeen. He had spells in the team in 1931 when the great Pittodrie scandal of that year broke out. Off the field, Dick was building his own empire; the family partnership of father and sons Herbert, James, Peter and Richard was adding more cinemas like The Globe, The King's and the Astoria. Dick returned to Pittodrie in 1946 and was voted on to the board three years later in August 1949. It was his business acumen, which was put to good use at Pittodrie. Dick had amassed a chain of cinemas in the city and he spent his time balancing his business commitments with ensuring that Aberdeen as a club rarely lived beyond their means. That sometimes prudent approach did not hinder progress both on and off the park at Pittodrie. The ground itself was developed to become the first all-seated, all-covered stadium in Britain and Dick Donald was behind those developments, which took Aberdeen to the forefront of the game in Britain. Dick was appointed chairman in 1970 and although Aberdeen were criticised in the 1970s for selling some of their prized assets including the likes of Martin Buchan and Joe Harper, Dick insisted that Aberdeen would be run with a prudence that clubs these days can only dream about. It was Dick Donald who, after losing manager Billy McNeill to Celtic in 1978, turned to sacked St Mirren boss Alex Ferguson to take over as Aberdeen manager. Donald identified the qualities required and the rest, as they say, is history. Had it not been for Dick's astute awareness all those years ago Aberdeen may not have gone on to achieve what they did. Alex Ferguson had always looked upon Dick Donald as a father figure during his glorious spell with the Dons and in the modern game you don't get much of a higher accolade than that.

SCOTLAND'S NUMBER ONE

Not many players hold the distinction of representing their country at four World Cups, but Jim Leighton did just that in 1982, 1986, 1990 and 1998. His early years involved a spell with Deveronvale and learning his trade under the great Bobby Clark. By 1978 Alex Ferguson chose Jim as replacement for the injured Clark for the season opener against Hearts at Tynecastle. It was a real test for the young keeper. Ninety minutes later Fergie knew he had a real talent in his midst. It was after the Dons' title success in 1980 that Jim was handed the number one jersey for keeps and that was the real beginning of an incredible success story. Jim Leighton won the first of a clutch of winners' medals when he was in the Aberdeen side that won the Scottish Cup at Hampden in 1982. It was the beginning of a golden age for the Dons and along with Alex McLeish and Willie Miller in front of him, the Dons defence with Jim Leighton went on to become the meanest in British football. It laid the foundation for success at both home and in Europe. It was October 13th 1982 that Jim earned the first of his 91 Scotland caps against East Germany at Hampden. Over the next 17 years Leighton amassed his record haul of caps, and his international career peaked in 1998 when he played for Scotland in the opening game of the World Cup in France against holders Brazil. In between times Leighton was in the Aberdeen team that won three Scottish Cups in succession, as well as the European Cup Winners' Cup and Super Cup in 1983. Two years later, and with successive Premier League championships in the bag, Aberdeen won the Scottish Cup again with Jim Leighton in the side in 1986 when the Dons cruised to a 3-0 win over Hearts. Two years later Jim followed Alex Ferguson to Manchester United and it was fair to suggest that Jim did not enjoy the best of times at Old Trafford. However, it was a measure of his character that he returned to Scotland and the international team during a spell with Hibernian. That prompted a return to Pittodrie when Roy Aitken brought Jim 'home' in 1997. A year later, Jim Leighton made his 500th competitive appearance for the Dons against Dundee United at Tannadice before eventually retiring to take over goalkeeper coaching duties at Pittodrie, a role which he holds to the present day.

MEDALLION MEN

Willie Miller and Alex McLeish head the all-time medals table at Aberdeen. The Dons legends racked up an incredible 24 winners' medals between them as Aberdeen enjoyed their most successful period in their history during the 1980s. The table below includes the Dons top 15 medal winners in the club's history.

Name	Years	Honours	Total
Willie Miller	1971-91	ECWC, ESC, Lge (3) SC (4) LC (3)	12
Alex McLeish	1976-94	ECWC, ESC, Lge (3) SC (5) LC (2)	12
Neale Cooper	1979-86	ECWC, ESC, Lge (2) SC (4) LC (1)	9
Jim Leighton	1978-87	ECWC, ESC, Lge (2) SC (4) LC (1)	9
Stewart McKimmie	1983-97	ESC, Lge (2) SC (3) LC (3)	9
Eric Black	1979-86	ECWC, ESC, Lge (2) SC (3) LC (1)	8
John Hewitt	1978-87	ECWC, ESC, Lge (2) SC (3) LC (1)	8
Neil Simpson	1978-89	ECWC, ESC, Lge (2) SC (3) LC (1)	8
Peter Weir	1981-87	ECWC, ESC, Lge (2) SC (3) LC (1)	8
Mark McGhee	1979-84	ECWC, ESC, Lge (2) SC (3) LC (1)	8
John McMaster	1971-86	ECWC, ESC, Lge (2) SC (2) LC (1)	7
Doug Rougvie	1971-84	ECWC, ESC, Lge (2) SC (3)	7
Gordon Strachan	1977-84	ECWC, ESC, Lge (2) SC (3)	7
Doug Bell	1979-86	ESC, Lge (2) SC (2) LC (1)	6
Billy Stark	1983-88	Lge (2) SC (2) LC (1)	5

Medal Table by Country of Origin and Nationality (All Players)

Scotland	96
England	1
Holland	3
Denmark	1
South Africa	2
Total	103

ECWC; European Cup Winners' Cup, ESC; European Super Cup, Lge; League, SC; Scottish Cup, LC; League Cup

DOUBLE TOPS

When Aberdeen retained the Scottish Premier League title in 1985, they achieved their success on the back of six double wins on away soil. The Dons defeated Dumbarton, Dundee, Hearts, Hibernian, Morton and Rangers on both away trips that season. Aberdeen also racked up home doubles against Dumbarton, Hibernian, Morton and St Mirren. The points tally of 59 was a new Premier League record. The Dons also conceded only 13 goals from their 18 away league matches. Aberdeen also scored 103 goals in 45 competitive matches that season with new signing Frank McDougall scoring 26 in his first season at Pittodrie.

PAYING THE PENALTY

On September 26th 1953, Aberdeen took on Celtic at Parkhead in what was the Dons' first stern test of their title credentials. However, it turned out to be a day to forget for Aberdeen captain Jimmy Mitchell. The £10,000 signing from Morton was caught out by the speedy Celtic front players and Mitchell conceded no less than three penalties in the game. Not surprisingly, Aberdeen went down 3-0 as all three penalties were converted.

TWO INTO FOUR FOR MATT

Matt Armstrong was a prolific scorer for Aberdeen in the 1930s. His partnership in attack with Willie Mills was one of the most feared in British football. On the final day of the 1933/34 season, Matt scored four goals in two matches. Apart from playing for Aberdeen reserves in the morning where he scored twice, Matt also turned out for the Aberdeen first team and scored both goals in a 2-2 draw with Queen's Park as the season drew to a close and the club had to complete their fixtures by that day.

CHEYNE GANG

Aberdeen and Scotland inside-forward Alex Cheyne was at his prolific best when Aberdeen beat Hibernian 4-2 at Pittodrie on September 10th 1927. Cheyne, of 'Hampden Roar' fame, scored a hat-trick in less than ten minutes. It was reported his teammates went out of their way to assist Cheyne to score his third, and the quickest hat-trick by an Aberdeen player at that time.

GENTLEMAN GEORGE

As Aberdeen legend George Hamilton was known during a memorable Pittodrie career. Hamilton had been a club record signing from Queen of the South in 1937 when Aberdeen paid £2,750 for his services. Hamilton went on to play 281 games for the club, scoring 153 goals, and apart from a short six-month spell with Hearts, it was at Pittodrie where Hamilton thrived. He was in the side that won the Southern League Cup, and Scottish Cup, just after the war and his final appearance for the club came when Aberdeen clinched their first league title in 1955. He got the nickname 'Gentleman' due to his superb sportsmanship and having only ever been booked once in his career. Hamilton remained at Pittodrie for a spell as he played in the successful reserve side where he passed on his experience to the younger Aberdeen players.

THE GREAT MYSTERY

On the morning of November 18th 1931 the club announced that five first-team players, Jimmy Black, Hugh McLaren, Frank Hill, Benny Yorston and David Galloway were dropped from the first team and that they would never play for the club again. It was a bombshell that was shrouded in mystery as the club refused to elaborate on their decision. Donald Colman had not long returned to the club as trainer and he had to deal with most of the unsavoury business. It became known locally as 'the Great Mystery' but many years later it was revealed that a half-time betting racket was uncovered. All five players were eventually sold within several months. Frank Hill went on to enjoy fame with Arsenal and Scotland, while record scorer Yorston joined Sunderland.

WILLIE MACAULAY

The first-ever Aberdeen captain that led his side out in the club's first matches in 1903. MacAulay had been an inspirational figure and it was fitting that he scored Aberdeen's first-ever goal in their opening match against Stenhousemuir. 'Mac', as he was known, joined Aberdeen from Middlesbrough in 1903 and he eventually relinquished the captaincy when Duncan McNicol arrived from Arsenal. He played 69 matches for the club, scoring 21 goals before joining Falkirk for £50 in 1906.

THAT'S FINAL

Aberdeen have appeared in 15 Scottish Cup finals, winning the trophy on seven occasions. The first final came in 1937 before a record 146,433 attendance as the Dons went down 2-1 to Celtic. The first success came ten years later against Hibernian. Aberdeen won the trophy three times in succession in 1982, 1983 and 1984, the first provincial club to do so that century. Aberdeen have beaten Hibernian, Celtic (three times), Rangers (twice) and Hearts in previous Scottish Cup finals. Aberdeen were also involved in the first-ever penalty shoot-out in the final when they defeated Celtic 9-8 on penalties in 1990 after the game finished 0-0.

ABERDEEN FC CUP FINAL APPEARANCES

Alex McLeish 6, Willie Miller 5, George Hamilton 4, Fred Martin 4, Jack Hather 4, John McMaster 4, Jim Leighton 4, Neale Cooper 4, Stewart McKimmie 4, Tony Harris 3, Jimmy Mitchell 3, Alex Young 3, Jack Allister 3, Paddy Buckley 3, Bobby Clark 3, Doug Rougvie 3, Gordon Strachan 3, Mark McGhee 3, Neil Simpson 3, John Hewitt 3, Eric Black 3, Peter Weir 3, George Johnstone 2, Frank Dunlop 2, Dave Shaw 2, Ian Rodger 2, Harry Yorston 2, Dave Caldwell 2, Archie Glen 2, Jim Clunie 2, Tom McMillan 2, Joe Harper 2, Stuart Kennedy 2, Doug Bell 2, Billy Stark 2, Jim Bett 2, Theo Snelders 2, Brian Grant 2, Brian Irvine 2, Paul Mason 2, Eoin Jess 2, Willie Cooper, Bob Temple, Eddie Falloon, George Thomson, Jack Benyon, John McKenzie, Matt Armstrong, Willie Mills, John Lang, Pat McKenna, George Taylor, Joe McLaughlin, Willie Waddell, Stan Williams, Archie Baird, Billy McCall, Graham Leggat, Jimmy Hogg, Ken Brownlee, Dickie Ewen, Norman Davidson, Hugh Baird, Bob Wishart, Jim Whyte, Ally Shewan, Frank Munro, Jens Petersen, Jimmy Wilson, Jimmy Smith, Jim Storrie, Harry Melrose, Dave Johnston, Henning Boel, George Murray, Jim Hermiston, Martin Buchan, Derek McKay, Dave Robb, Jim Forrest, Arthur Graham, Steve Ritchie, Willie Garner, Dom Sullivan, Ian Fleming, Drew Jarvie, Duncan Davidson, Ian Scanlon, Andy Watson, Tom McQueen, Frank McDougall, Joe Miller, David Robertson, Charlie Nicholas, Bobby Connor, Hans Gillhaus, Graham Watson, Stephen Wright, Lee Richardson, Scott Booth, Duncan Shearer, Mixu Paatelainen, Gary Smith, one appearance each.

STEADY EDDIE

Back in 1965 when Aberdeen were struggling in the league and being embarrassed in the Scottish Cup, the arrival of a new manager heralded a new era at the club. Not many Aberdeen supporters would have been cracking open the champagne when the new manager was announced but that was soon to change when Eddie Turnbull took over as manager. Eddie quickly set about hauling the club out of their slumber and the early days were tough, but soon the players realised what was required and Eddie Turnbull began to instil some belief in to the side. Born in Falkirk on April 12th 1923, Eddie began his career with Grangemouth before joining Hibernian after the war. It was at Easter Road that he found success as a player and was part of the 'Famous Five' Hibernian front line that helped them to win three championships in the 1950s. Eddie won the first of his eight caps against Belgium in 1948. After retiring from playing in 1959 Turnbull remained at Easter Road as trainer but he severed his ties with the club in March 1963 and took his first steps in to coaching with Queen's Park. It was his revolutionary and visionary approach that attracted Aberdeen's interest and after Eddie took over from Tommy Pearson in February 1965 it was the start of a new era for Aberdeen. No less than 17 players were released as Turnbull wielded the axe and set up a new scouting network. The signs of recovery were almost instant and in 1967 the Dons were never quite the same in the cup final against Celtic without their manager present who was confined to his hotel sickbed. Without doubt Eddie's finest hour as Aberdeen manager came in 1970 when he masterminded a sensational win over Celtic in the Scottish Cup final. The Dons went in to the game as rank outsiders but the ring of confidence that Eddie had always believed in came good on the day. Two weeks before the final Eddie took his side down to Celtic Park for a league game which was viewed as a dress rehearsal. If Celtic had won that night then the title would be staying at Parkhead. Aberdeen won 2-1 in what was seen as a huge shock at the time but the victory gave Aberdeen confidence for the final. It all climaxed with a memorable return to the city before a welcome from almost 100,000 of the citizens of Aberdeen.

JIMMY JIMMY

Aberdeen turned to Dunfermline manager Jimmy Calderwood in their time of need in 2004. After a disastrous spell under the troubled Steve Paterson, Aberdeen brought the experienced Calderwood to the club, along with assistant Jimmy Nicholl. Calderwood and his team were to remain at Pittodrie for five seasons – the longest period any manager had stayed with the club since Alex Ferguson – before parting company in May 2009 after leading the club back into Europe. Calderwood produced a side that was as consistent as any previous Aberdeen time with five consecutive top-six placings. However, a shocking sequence of results in the domestic cup competitions was eventually to prove decisive as the Aberdeen board decided a new face was required to take the club forward.

LIONS TOO MUCH FOR DANDIES

The 'Dandy' Dons, as the old rosettes declared, marched on to the 1967 Scottish Cup Final in impressive fashion. After hammering Dundee and St. Johnstone 5-0 in the opening two rounds, the Dons were held by Hibernian in the quarter-final after a 1-1 draw at Easter Road before a 37,200 crowd. The Pittodrie replay attracted a record midweek attendance of 44,000 as the Dons won 3-0 to go through. After beating Dundee United in the semi-final at Dens Park, Aberdeen fell in the final against Celtic who were on the threshold of European success and their renowned 'Lisbon Lions' team.

DONS DOWN DUNS

Aberdeen's record score away from home in a competitive fixture was an emphatic 8-0 win over non-league Duns in the 1954 Scottish Cup. While there was much interest in the Borders area over the tie, Aberdeen were keen to get the game out of the way. The tie was effectively played on a mudbath of a pitch with the ground barely suitable for such an important game. Paddy Buckley made light of the conditions and helped himself to four goals. The tiny crowd of 700 also included six Aberdeen supporters who made the 12-hour round trip by car. Aberdeen only received six requests for tickets before the tie. The Dons went on to reach the final later that season only to go down to Celtic after beating Rangers emphatically in the semi.

EUROPEAN CHAMPIONS CUP

Aberdeen first appeared in Europe's premier competition in 1980, some 25 years too late in the opinion of many. Back in 1955, as Aberdeen won the league title, they naively assumed that they would represent Scotland in the new European Cup which was to start from 1955/56. However, as the inaugural competition was by each national association nominating any club, the loophole was exploited to the full by the SFA who put Hibernian forward to represent Scotland. With Hibernian chairman Harry Swan also president of the SFA at that time, Aberdeen as Scottish champions were treated very poorly. When Aberdeen finally took their bow they opened with a 1-0 win over Austrian champions Vienna at Pittodrie on September 17th 1980. After losing out to Liverpool in the next round, Aberdeen went on to play eight further ties in the European Cup. The furthest the Dons reached was the quarter-finals in 1986 when they went out to Gothenburg on away goals.

CAPTAIN COOL

As Martin Buchan was remembered by the Pittodrie faithful. Aberdeen-born Buchan emerged as a player of real class in 1966 after joining the club from Banks O'Dee in 1965. Buchan developed under Eddie Turnbull and he became the first 'sweeper' in Scottish football; a defensive 'last man' as was so popular in European football. Buchan epitomised calm in the Aberdeen defence that created a British record in 1971. Later that year he was named as the Scottish Writers' Player of the Year and also earned his first Scotland cap. Buchan became the youngest-ever captain to lift the Scottish Cup in 1970, at 21 years of age. In February 1972 he joined Manchester United in a record £125,000 deal. In 1977 he completed a remarkable double as he led Manchester United to FA Cup glory at Wembley. Buchan was rewarded with a testimonial from the Old Trafford club in 1983 and it was fitting that Aberdeen would supply the opposition for his big day. Almost 30,000 turned out at Old Trafford to see Aberdeen parade the European Cup Winners' Cup before drawing 2-2 with United. Buchan went on to make 192 appearances for Aberdeen, scoring eleven goals. After spells playing for Oldham Athletic, and managing Burnley, Buchan retired from the game. He currently works for the PFA in England.

ANGLO DONS

Long before the English Premier flexed its considerable power, the trail from Pittodrie to England has been a long one. One of the first high-profile transfers was that of Alec Jackson who was sold to Huddersfield Town in 1924 after only one amazing season at Pittodrie. Jackson went on to become one of the famous 'Wembley Wizards' of 1928; the Scottish side that humiliated England at Wembley with Jackson scoring a hat-trick. Jock Hutton – the burly Aberdeen full-back who was sold to Blackburn Rovers for a club record £6,000 in 1926 – was already a Scotland international before his move to Lancashire. In the 1950s there were very few Aberdeen players who went south, mainly due to the wage restrictions that were in place in England as top Scottish league players could earn more than their counterparts down south. That all changed in the 1960s and among the Aberdeen players who were sold included; George Kinnell, Doug Coutts and George Mulhall. Aberdeen also parted company with established stars like Martin Buchan to Manchester United in 1972 for £125,000 and Joe Harper to Everton for £172,000. In 1980 Tottenham paid a club record £800,000 for Steve Archibald. The record sale to an English club was that of Eoin Jess to Coventry for £1.75m in 1996.

MIND YOUR HEAD

On March 21st 1908 Aberdeen reached their first Scottish Cup semi-final only to lose 1-0 to Celtic at Pittodrie. A record 20,000 crowd filled every vantage point in the ground. The game itself did not pass without incident as aggressive tactics deployed by the visitors infuriated the home support. With several decisions not going Aberdeen's way, the referee came in for fierce criticism. At full-time there was no hiding place as the Celtic players were pelted with stones after the game as the players attempted to leave the field.

DONS ALL WASHED UP

Manchester United visited Aberdeen for a holiday friendly on September 25th 1950. The game was postponed for 24 hours as torrential rain and gale force winds battered the Aberdeen area. When the teams finally played the game, it was a whirlwind response from United who incredibly won 5-3 after Aberdeen had raced into a three-goal lead.

MEDAL FOR COOPER

Aberdeen stalwart Willie Cooper gave the club 20 years of service before he missed the 1947 cup final through injury in what was the twilight of his career. Cooper had scored a rare goal that had set Aberdeen on their way to Hampden in the opening round win over Partick Thistle. The Aberdeen full-back joined the team on the Hampden pitch as the cup was presented to Frank Dunlop. Later the Aberdeen legend received a medal as the SFA broke with a long-standing tradition and allowed Cooper to collect his winners' gong.

FIRST CELTIC VISIT TO ABERDEEN

Glasgow rivals Celtic have been, by tradition, one of the toughest opponents for Aberdeen through the years. Founded in 1888, their first visit to Aberdeen came on August 16th 1889 when Celtic were invited by Victoria United to play them in what was Victoria's first-ever outing. Celtic ran out comfortable 10-0 winners at the Recreation Grounds in the south side of the town. Included in that Victoria side was Peter Simpson, who went on to become the first trainer at Aberdeen in 1903. Victoria United would go on to be part of the amalgamation that formed the present Aberdeen Football Club in April 1903.

HALLIDAY HAS HIS DAY

Dave Halliday ended his association with the Dons in July 1955 by agreeing to take over at Leicester City. Halliday joined Aberdeen as manager in 1937 after excelling at non-league Yeovil Town. After leading Aberdeen to a first league title in 1955, Halliday had won the Southern League Cup and Scottish Cup and his record is only bettered by Alex Ferguson. It was in the immediate aftermath of that title success that Halliday shocked the club by announcing that he was taking over at Leicester City. There were other factors involved; an unsavoury dispute over a player's bonus payment for winning the title soured relations, while Aberdeen being passed over by the SFA to enter the new European Cup prevented the Dons manager from taking the club further.

146,433

The record attendance at a British club game was when Aberdeen clashed with Celtic at Hampden on April 24th 1937. It was also reported that around 10,000 gained entry to the ground by 'other means', while an estimated 20,000 were locked out. Thousands also approached the Hampden area only to turn back. An estimated 30,000 made the journey down from Aberdeen for the final by all manner of means with special trains and cars. Several supporters set off two days ahead of the game, cycling to Glasgow.

SUNDAY BEST TOO MUCH FOR KEEGAN

By tradition Aberdeen have always relished the chance to put one over visiting English teams, whether it be in friendly or competitive matches. In 1981 the Dons hosted their own pre-season tournament as Manchester United, West Ham United and Southampton came north for the two-day event. Aberdeen dismissed West Ham 3-0 before taking on Kevin Keegan and Southampton on the Sunday after they had eased past Manchester United. The Saints had no answer to Aberdeen who hammered their guests 5-1 to lift their own inaugural trophy in front of their own support.

CENTURIANS

While Aberdeen celebrated their centenary in 2003 with a glamour friendly against Liverpool at Pittodrie, the Dons have also returned the favour for many clubs in the past. Most notable perhaps was the Dons' visit to Filbert Street in August 1984 to play Leicester City to commemorate their 100 years in existence. Other sides that Aberdeen have played to mark centenaries include Bradford City, Dunfermline Athletic, Montrose, Arbroath and several Highland League clubs.

EVERTON WERE THE FIRST

Everton became the first English team to visit Aberdeen, winning 3-1 in a Pittodrie friendly on April 30th 1901. The Goodison Park club were also visitors to Aberdeen in 1956, 1997 and in 2006 for Russell Anderson's testimonial. Aberdeen also met the Merseyside club in Canada in the summer of 1956 while both clubs were on tour.

FORMER PLAYERS' ASSOCIATION

Aberdeen set up a Former Players' Association on the back of a successful centenary year in November 2003. Former players Duncan Davidson, Jimmy Wilson and Ally Shewan head up the committee that looks after all former players of the club.

LEAGUE DECIDERS

"The success of Aberdeen in establishing themselves as a threat to the Old Firm has been a great boost to the game. If we do lose our title then there will be no more worthy successors than Aberdeen." The words of the great Jock Stein as Celtic manager in April 1971 before Aberdeen clashed with Celtic at Pittodrie in what was effectively a title decider. Going into the game Aberdeen were three points ahead, but with two more games played, so a victory for the Dons would all but guarantee the championship. A 1-1 draw left the Dons dreaming of what might have been. Arthur Graham rounded Celtic keeper Williams in the second half only to see his effort cleared off the line by Billy McNeill. In May 1991 it was a different story as Aberdeen lost 2-0 to Rangers on the last day of the season. Had Aberdeen taken a point or more, then the title would have gone to Pittodrie. The Dons suffered through having to use four different keepers that season, the last of which was young rookie Michael Watt who was thrown into the Ibrox cauldron on that last day.

DRYBROUGH CUP CHEERS

Sponsorship in the shape of the imposing Drybrough Cup came to Scottish football in 1971. Aberdeen were the first and last winners of the solid silver cup which was almost three feet high. Aberdeen won the competition in 1971 after beating East Fife (3-0) and Airdrie (4-1), both away from home, to qualify for the final. A 28,000 crowd gathered at Pittodrie for the first final between Aberdeen and Celtic in what was seen as the perfect curtain-raiser to the new football season. Goals from Dave Robb and Joe Harper gave the Dons a deserved 2-1 win over their great rivals. The cup was open to the top-four scoring sides in the top two divisions from the previous season. Aberdeen won the last competition in 1980 with a 2-1 win over St Mirren at Hampden.

NORTHERN LEAGUE

The now defunct Northern League formed in 1891 to be competed for by clubs from the Aberdeen, Tayside and Fife areas. This was the first league set up that the original Aberdeen FC had competed in. It was not until 1905 that Aberdeen actually won the league and, ironically, it was their reserve side that won the title as Aberdeen by that time had amalgamated and become part of mainstream Scottish football. The original trophy is still in place in the Pittodrie boardroom.

HIBEES HERE?

In November 1902 Aberdeen resisted an attempt by Edinburgh-based Hibernian to take over the club and relocate to the north-east. Hibernian had seen Aberdeen as an ideal location due to a significant population base with no recognised league football at that time. The Aberdeen board, and manager Jimmy Phillip in particular, resisted the overtures and the developments moved the amalgamation process closer to reality.

DONS FIRST DARK BLUE

Willie Lennie became the first Aberdeen player to be capped for Scotland when he turned out against Wales at Dens Park on March 7th 1908. Lennie scored the Scots' late winner in a 2-1 win. A week later Lennie came up against teammate Charlie O'Hagan as Scotland played Ireland. O'Hagan was the Irish captain on that occasion. Lennie went on to become a huge favourite at Pittodrie and he was the first Aberdeen player to receive a benefit match from the club in January 1910.

SUPER BENNY YORSTON

Born in Nigg, Benny Yorston scored 38 goals from 38 league matches in 1929/30; a club record that still stands to this day. Yorston also scored six in the Scottish Cup to create a highest total in any one season by an Aberdeen player. Yorston began his career at Montrose but it was during Aberdeen's tour to South Africa in 1927 that he emerged as a player of genuine class. Yorston was also capped for Scotland before his Aberdeen career was cut short by his involvement in the 'Great Mystery' of 1931.

HIGH FIVE

Seen more as a novelty than anything else, the first Aberdeen side to compete in an official five-a-side tournament was the team of 1970 that competed in the Daily Express National Championships at Wembley in November of that year. Steve Murray, Bobby Clark, Jim Hamilton, Jim Forrest, Joe Harper and Jim Hermiston made up the Dons side that competed against the best in England in the 16-team tournament. Aberdeen lost out to West Ham United in one of the opening games. Aberdeen would return in later years on occasion after domestic success in Scotland prompted invitations from the English sponsors. In 1985, Scottish brewery company Tennent's were behind the new 'Sixes' football that was played indoors over the winter. Aberdeen were the inaugural winners of the competition that lasted into the early 1990s.

FIRST RECORD ATTENDANCE

The visit of Clyde on November 12th 1904 attracted a first record attendance at Pittodrie of 12,000 paying the princely sum of £284 gate receipts. The game was the semi-final of the Qualifying Cup as Aberdeen went on to win 1-0 to reach the final. The previous best attendance was for the first international played in Aberdeen in 1900.

EURO TRICKS

Frank Munro and Mark McGhee are the only Aberdeen players who have scored hat-tricks for the club in European football. Munro scored the Dons' first-ever goal in European competition when Aberdeen hammered KR Reykjavik 10-0 at Pittodrie on September 6th 1967. Mark McGhee scored his three in an incredible European Cup Winners' Cup quarter-final second leg at Pittodrie on March 21st 1984 against Hungarian side Ujpest Dozsa. Aberdeen trailed 2-0 from the first game and McGhee scored his second with minutes remaining to take the tie into extra time. The Aberdeen striker rounded off a superb night's work by scoring his third goal to put Aberdeen through to the semi-finals for the second time in their history. McGhee's first goal against Ujpest was also another landmark for Aberdeen as it was the Dons' 100th goal in European competition.

LEAGUE WINNERS

Outside of Celtic and Rangers, it is Aberdeen who share the most championships with both Hibernian and Hearts, with four titles each. While two of the Hearts championship wins came in the 19th century, Hibernian last took the title in 1952 three years before the first Aberdeen success. Aberdeen are the last club outside of the Old Firm to win the league, in 1985.

1885 AND ALL THAT

The original Aberdeen FC came into being in 1881 and it took the area several years before any organised football could be played. The introduction of the Aberdeenshire Cup and subsequent league in 1887 was the result of many clubs emerging in the town through the various works and clubs in Aberdeen. By 1885 the following clubs were playing regularly in the Aberdeen area: Aberdeen, Orion, Carlton, Aberdeen Rovers, Bon Accord, Gladstone, Our Boys, Alpine, Eldon, Alliance, Aberdeen Grammar, Granite City and Reform.

SCOTTISH CUP GOALS

Charlie 'Chattie' Mackie had the distinction of scoring Aberdeen's first-ever goal in the Scottish Cup against Alloa on January 23rd 1904 before he joined Manchester United. Three Aberdeen players have scored five goals in one tie; W. D. Nichol v Forfar 25/2/1911, Norman Davidson v Brechin City 3/2/1960 and Bobby Cummings v Clyde on 31/1/1962. Willie Grant scored four against Peterhead on 10/2/1923 in what was the Dons' record score of 13-0 in the Scottish Cup. Latterly, Benny Yorston, Paddy Buckley and Steve Archibald have also scored four for the Dons in a cup tie. Other landmark goals include;

200th Goal ... Jackie Benyon v Dundee 3/2/1934 .... SC 2nd round
300th Goal ... Tommy Pearson v Hearts 11/2/1950 .... SC 2nd round
400th Goal ... Norman Davidson v Third Lanark 8/4/1959 ..... SC SF replay
500th Goal ... Joe Harper v Celtic 11/4/1970 .... SC Final
600th Goal ... Eric Black v Rangers 21/5/1983 .... SC Final
700th Goal ... Hicham Zerouali v St Mirren 29/1/2000 .... SC 3rd round

EARLY LANDMARKS

The original Aberdeen FC struggled to gain any kind of momentum in their efforts to establish 'the dribbling game' in the north-east. Twelve people gathered for the first meeting on October 8th 1881. On November 4th Mr A. V. Lothian was appointed as president of the club. On December 15th 1881, nine new members were admitted. On February 14th 1882 the club applied for membership to the Scottish Football Association. By March of that year the club membership had risen to 22.

TOP MEN

Willie Miller has played the most games for Aberdeen in their history. The table below shows the top-ten player appearances for the club. The table contains appearances in league, Scottish Cup, League Cup and European matches only.

1	Willie Miller	1971-1991	797
2	Alex McLeish	1976-1994	693
3	Bobby Clark	1965-1980	594
4	Stewart McKimmie	1983-1997	561
5	Jim Leighton	1977-2000*	529
6	Drew Jarvie	1972-1982	386
7	Brian Irvine	1985-1997	384
8	Eoin Jess	1988-2001*	379
9	Willie Cooper	1927-1948	373
10	John Hewitt	1979-1989	364

Two spells with the club

Several other Aberdeen players have made 300 or more appearances for the club; Bert MacLachlan, Jackie Hather, Donald Colman, Dave Robb, Jim Bett, Jimmy Smith, Stuart Kennedy, Brian Grant, John McMaster, Neil Simpson, Jock Hume, Billy Little, Ally Shewan and Joe Harper*.

HOCKEY STICKS

Pittodrie hosted a hockey international on Saturday March 19th 1910 when 2,000 turned out to see England defeat Scotland 3-0.

PREMIER LEAGUE RECORD

Season	Lge	P	W	D	L	F	A	Pt	Pos.
1975/76	Prem	36	11	10	15	49	50	32	7th
1976/77	Prem	36	16	11	9	56	42	43	3rd
1977/78	Prem	36	22	9	5	68	29	53	2nd
1978/79	Prem	36	13	14	9	59	36	40	4th
1979/80	Prem	36	19	10	7	68	36	48	1st
1980/81	Prem	36	19	11	6	61	26	49	2nd
1981/82	Prem	36	23	7	6	71	29	53	2nd
1982/83	Prem	36	25	5	6	76	24	55	3rd
1983/84	Prem	36	25	7	4	78	21	57	1st
1984/85	Prem	36	27	5	4	89	26	59	1st
1985/86	Prem	36	16	12	8	62	31	44	4th
1986/87	Prem	44	21	16	7	63	29	58	4th
1987/88	Prem	44	20	17	7	55	26	57	4th
1988/89	Prem	36	18	14	4	51	25	50	2nd
1989/90	Prem	36	17	10	9	56	33	44	2nd
1990/91	Prem	36	22	9	5	62	27	53	2nd
1991/92	Prem	44	17	14	13	55	42	48	6th
1992/93	Prem	44	27	10	7	87	36	64	2nd
1993/94	Prem	44	17	21	6	58	36	55	2nd
1994/95	Prem	36	10	11	15	43	46	41	9th
1995/96	Prem	36	16	7	13	52	45	55	3rd
1996/97	Prem	36	10	12	14	45	54	42	6th
1997/98	Prem	36	9	12	15	39	53	39	6th
1998/99	Prem	36	10	7	19	43	71	37	8th
1999/00	SPL	36	9	6	21	44	83	33	10th
2000/01	SPL	38	11	12	15	45	52	45	7th
2001/02	SPL	38	16	7	15	51	49	55	4th
2002/03	SPL	38	13	10	15	41	54	49	8th
2003/04	SPL	38	9	7	22	39	63	34	11th
2004/05	SPL	38	18	7	13	44	39	61	4th
2005/06	SPL	38	13	15	10	46	40	54	6th
2006/07	SPL	38	19	8	11	55	38	65	3rd
2007/08	SPL	38	15	8	15	50	58	53	4th
2008/09	SPL	38	14	11	13	41	40	53	4th

MARK MCGHEE

One of Alex Ferguson's first signings for the Dons back in March 1979 was Mark McGhee when Aberdeen paid Newcastle United £70,000 for his services. McGhee had begun his career with Morton and his scoring exploits had attracted the attention of Newcastle. While McGhee took his time to settle at Pittodrie, he went on to become an integral part of the side that swept all before them at home, and in Europe. He also had the distinction of scoring the Dons' first-ever goal in the European Champions Cup in 1980 against Austria Vienna and it was his cross that led to John Hewitt scoring the goal that took the European Cup Winners' Cup to Pittodrie in 1983. Mark was also in the Aberdeen side that won the European Super Cup in December 1983. He scored one of the goals against SV Hamburg which prompted a move to the German club in 1984 after McGhee signed off by scoring the winning goal in the 1984 Scottish Cup Final for Aberdeen against Celtic – his last game for the Dons. A week later he scored for Scotland against England at Hampden in a 1-1 draw. McGhee returned to Pittodrie as manager, taking over from Jimmy Calderwood, in June 2009.

WELCOME PETERHEAD

The nearest senior team to Aberdeen are relative newcomers Peterhead who joined the Scottish League after being a prominent force in Highland League circles for many years. Situated at the north-east point of the country, Peterhead will more than likely always be remembered for a record 13-0 Scottish Cup defeat against Aberdeen in 1923. However, the teams actually first met on March 21st 1885 in what was Peterhead's first-ever game. Aberdeen won 4-0 at the Links in Peterhead. Two weeks later the new club won for the first time in a 2-1 win over Aberdeen Rovers.

ABERDEENSHIRE FA

The formation of the Aberdeenshire Football Association took place on April 18th 1887 as Dr F. Maitland-Moir later presented the association with a trophy to be played for by all member clubs – the Aberdeenshire Cup. The first-ever Aberdeenshire Cup final was played before a 1,000 crowd at the Chanonry on March 24th 1888. Aberdeen defeat Aberdeen Rangers 7-1.

PLAYER AND BOSS: MARK McGHEE WITH GORDON STRACHAN

ABERDEEN SCOTTISH CUP FINAL ATTENDANCES

1937 v Celtic, 147,365; 1947 v Hibernian, 82,140; 1953 v Rangers, 129,861; 1953 (replay) v Rangers, 112,619; 1954 v Celtic, 129,926; 1959 v St Mirren, 108,591; 1967 v Celtic, 127,117; 1970 v Celtic, 108,244; 1978 v Rangers, 61,563; 1982 v Rangers, 53,788; 1983 v Rangers, 62,979; 1984 v Celtic, 58,900; 1986 v Hearts, 62,841; 1990 v Celtic, 60,493; 1993 v Rangers, 50,715; 2000 v Rangers, 50,865.

WINTER BLUES

The team failed to turn up for their league meeting with Hearts at Tynecastle on December 29th 1906. As usual the team travelled south by train but the poor weather conditions meant that the train was snowbound in Forfar and unable to continue the journey. The SFA were unsympathetic to the Dons' plight and promptly fined the club for not fulfilling a fixture. Three weeks later Aberdeen were humiliated in the Scottish Cup as they went down to non-league Johnstone. The conditions in the Renfrew ground were abysmal and Aberdeen lodged a protest after the game, claiming that the pitch was not suitable and 'not square'. Their protest was thrown out by the SFA to compound a miserable month for the club.

GETTING SHIRTY

A common sight these days is to see players whip off their shirts by way of a celebration before the mandatory yellow card. In September 1975, Aberdeen centre-half Willie Young was far from in celebratory mood as he was substituted during a game against Dundee United at Pittodrie. Not one for standing on ceremony, the big defender ripped off his shirt and launched it towards the Aberdeen dugout. Young was soon transferred to Tottenham Hotspur in a £125,000 deal. Young was no stranger to controversy as he was also one of the 'Copenhagen Five' Scotland players who were involved in some nightclub bother while away with Scotland on under-23 duty. He is also one of the few players who crossed the great north London divide by joining Arsenal after a spell with Spurs.

MAGICAL MAGYAR OR MERCENARY?

One player who would never pick up a loyalty bonus but nevertheless left a lasting impression at Pittodrie was Hungarian international Zoltan Varga. Varga had a colourful past, to say the least, as he was involved in a betting scandal that rocked German football to the core and his subsequent ban in Germany left the door open for Aberdeen to bring him to Scotland in October 1972 for a £40,000 fee from Hertha Berlin. Varga was an established Hungarian international with a natural ability that was almost alien to the Scottish game at that time. There was also a novelty value in that, by tradition, Aberdeen never signed foreign players. Varga had been in exile for almost a year and his Dons debut came against Falkirk at Pittodrie on October 14th 1972. Aberdeen had eventually obtained the necessary international clearance to allow him to play. Varga not surprisingly had a very quiet match but he at least showed glimpses of his talent with some fine touches and ball control. In midfield he was soon to make his mark and many observers at the time suggested that Varga was always a couple of moves ahead of his opponents and teammates alike. While Varga certainly took his time to ease himself back into playing it was Aberdeen's Ian Taylor who saved the Dons blushes by scoring both goals in a 2-2 draw against Falkirk. Aberdeen even had a Joe Harper penalty saved just before half-time and it took until seven minutes from time before the Dons squared the game. Earlier Falkirk had taken the lead for a second time after Alec Willoughby put through his own net. Included in the Falkirk side was a young Stuart Kennedy who would later join Aberdeen as did Jim Shirra in 1976.

Zoltan Varga Factfile

Date of Birth: 1.1.1945
Born: Val, Hungary
Signed: October 1972
Aberdeen Appearances: 31
Aberdeen Goals: 10
International Details: 16 youth internationals, 3 under-23 appearances,
15 full international appearances for Hungary
Other Clubs: Hertha Berlin, Ferencvaros, Ajax, Borussia Dortmund.

SCOTLAND AT PITTODRIE

Hampden Park has been the traditional home for the national team since Scotland played England at the first Hampden in 1878. The present Aberdeen FC had not yet seen the light of day when Scotland played Wales at the new ground at Pittodrie in 1900. The Scottish side included seven Rangers players and a record attendance of 12,000 turned up for the first full international in the Granite City. Scotland won 5-2 with goals from Bell, Hamilton (2), Wilson and Smith. In 1921 the Welsh returned and Scotland triumphed again, winning 2-1 with two goals from Andy Wilson. A crowd of 20,824 paid £2,353 for the privilege. Pittodrie had, by that time, a new stand which could house up to 1,000 spectators. In 1934, Scotland completed a hat-trick of wins over the Welsh at Pittodrie when Aberdonian Dally Duncan scored one of the Scots' goals in an exciting 3-2 victory. Three years later Ireland drew 1-1 with the Scots in what was to be the last international at Pittodrie for many years. Scotland broke with tradition in 1971 when the European Championship tie against Belgium was taken to Pittodrie in an effort to intimidate the tough Belgians. Scotland had played 74 consecutive internationals at Hampden prior to the Pittodrie tie and 36,500 fans packed the ground to see the Scots battle to a deserved 1-0 win. Scotland's preparations for Italia 1990 were in the final stages as Egypt visited Pittodrie in 1990. On that occasion a slick Egyptian side won 3-1. This was the first Pittodrie defeat for the national side. With the World Cup in 1994 going to the USA, the Scots were still in contention for a place in the finals when Estonia visited in 1993. A comfortable 3-1 win was marred by a Pittodrie crowd who were in no mood to show national fervour towards the only Rangers player in the side, Ian Ferguson. Three months later, Scotland welcomed Switzerland in what was a must win situation for the Scots. The Swiss had forced themselves into pole position and were well worthy of a 1-1 draw before a capacity Pittodrie crowd. The new Richard Donald Stand was in place for this match that was made all the more atmospheric by the large and colourful Swiss support. In 1997, Belarus were well beaten in a 4-1 win before Nigeria beat Scotland in 2002. Up until that point the only Pittodrie defeats were against African opposition. The trend was ended in the last Scotland visit to Pittodrie against South Africa in 2007.

SCOTLAND INTERNATIONALS AT PITTODRIE

3/2/1900 ......Scotland 5:2 Wales (Bell, Hamilton 2, Wilson, Smith). 12,000
12/2/1921 ....Scotland 2:1 Wales (Wilson 2)..20,824
21/3/1934 ....Scotland 3:2 Wales (Duncan, Napier 2).........................26,334
10/11/1937 ..Scotland 1:1 Ireland (Smith)..21,878
10/11/1971 ..Scotland 1:0 Belgium (O'Hare) 36,500
16/5/1990 ....Scotland 1:3 Egypt (McCoist) 23,000
2/6/1993 ......Scotland 3:1 Estonia (McClair, Nevin 2) 14,500
8/9/1993 ......Scotland 1:1 Switzerland (Collins) 21,500
7/9/1997 ......Scotland 4:1 Belarus (Gallacher 2, Hopkin 2)...............20,160
14/10/1998 ..Scotland 2:1 Faroe Isles (Burley, Dodds).......................16,500
17/4/2002 ....Scotland 1:2 Nigeria (Dailly) 20,465
22/8/2007 ....Scotland 1:0 South Africa (Boyd) 13,723

SCOTLAND UNDER-23 INTERNATIONALS AT PITTODRIE

28/2/1962 ....Scotland 2:4 England (Hunter, Hughes) 26,000
6/12/1962 ....Scotland 2:0 Wales (Smith, Jeffrey)................................22,000
24/2/1965 ....Scotland 0:0 England 25,000
14/1/1970 ....Scotland 1:1 Wales (O'Hare)..15,349
26/1/1972 ....Scotland 2:0 Wales (Jardine, Macari) 15,000
27/2/1974 ....Scotland 3:0 Wales 6,000

SCOTLAND UNDER-21 INTERNATIONALS AT PITTODRIE

17/9/1978 ....Scotland 3:1 USA (Melrose, Orr, MacLeod) 6,500
4/3/1980 ......Scotland 0:0 England 19,000
18/11/1980 ..Scotland 2:1 Denmark (Watson, Gillespie)....................11,000
24/3/1982 ....Scotland 0:0 Italy..20,000
14/3/1984 ....Scotland 2:1 Yugoslavia (Johnston, McClair)................17,000
16/2/1988 ....Scotland 0:1 England 23,000
24/3/1992 ....Scotland 4:3 Germany (Creaney,Rae,Lambert,McKinnon)....
....22,000
22/4/1992 ....Scotland 0:0 Sweden..22,000
1/9/2006 ......Scotland 1:3 France (Adam)..11,950

SOUTH TERRACE

It was seen, at the time, as the final piece in the Pittodrie jigsaw when the cantilever roof was built over the South Terrace at Pittodrie in the summer of 1980. For many years the gradual improvements that had been made at the ground had brought Pittodrie to the forefront of stadia in the country. In the days before the enforced changes as a result of the tragedies at Heysel and Bradford, Pittodrie was seen as the model of what a modern ground should aspire to; comfort, safety and also retaining the atmosphere, which were seen as the important factors. While Pittodrie these days may be looking a bit dated, back then it attracted widespread attention when it became the first all-seated stadium in Britain in 1978 and two years later the first all-covered and all-seated ground after completion of the cantilever roof. Work began almost immediately after the Dons had clinched the Premier League championship in May 1980. The bench style seats that were in place would remain for the next year before they were replaced by individual seating which allowed season tickets to be purchased there for the first time in 1981. The top nine rows of seating and the old terracing had to be removed to allow space for the 14 pylons which had to be excavated to a depth of 100ft to be strong enough to sustain the new roof which would extend to almost the side of the pitch. The reason that the roof was not extended further was the concern that natural sunlight would not be able to reach all areas of the playing surface. Apart from the new roof itself, the area had to be totally restructured to allow for new access stairs to be installed as well as a new television gantry, shops and toilets. The construction of the roof also brought with it a fantastic atmosphere inside the stadium with all four sides now covered. Not all of the terracing could be reinstated which cut the capacity down to allow for a new walkway at the rear of the stand. Work was completed in time for Aberdeen to launch their new season as champions and also play their first-ever European Champions Cup tie that season. The first game played in front of the new roof was a Drybrough Cup opener against Airdrie when Aberdeen eased to a 4-1 win before being officially opened a week later against Arsenal.

IN THE HOT SEAT

The demise of Aberdeen since the heady days of the 1980s is clearly indicated in the fortunes of previous Aberdeen managers. While Billy McNeill's one season in charge returned a high percentage of success, the real success was achieved under Alex Ferguson during his incredible seven years at Pittodrie. Former Celtic legend McNeill came close to winning a league and cup double in season 1977/78, but it was not until Ferguson arrived that Aberdeen began to achieve regular success. The fact that Aberdeen had only three managers in their first 50 years of existence reflects the changing nature of the game. The arrival of Eddie Turnbull in 1965 provided a huge change in approach from the manager's role at Pittodrie. Up until that point, the more reserved and dignified approach by the likes of Jimmy Philip and Dave Halliday was accepted back then. The game in Scotland was catching on to the more revolutionary, and ultimately successful, approach by many European clubs. Turnbull was perhaps the first 'tracksuit' Dons manager as he spent more time on the training field than in the tight confines of the manager's office. That trend has continued and developed in the modern era. By tradition, Aberdeen as a club had a record of sticking by their various managers in the past. It was only in the post-Ferguson era where demands changed dramatically that this loyal approach changed. Jimmy Philip, the first-ever Aberdeen manager retired in 1924, while Pat Travers called time on his 14-year spell at Pittodrie by moving closer to his roots with Clyde. Dave Halliday was tempted to join ailing Leicester City after he secured a first-ever league title for the Dons in 1955. It was the Dons not being put forward by the SFA to represent Scotland in the new European Cup that also had a bearing on his decision to move. It was only when Dave Shaw reverted to his favoured trainer's role in 1959 as Tommy Pearson took over that the first Aberdeen manager was seen as under-achieving. In recent times the pressures of the modern game are reflected in the changes that have been made at Pittodrie. Every manager since that near-catastrophic season of 1994/95 has failed to deliver what was required to keep Aberdeen at the top end of the game in Scottish football. While expectations remained high, the most calming influence came during Jimmy Calderwood's tenure as regular top-half finishes were supplemented by a return to European football before he was replaced by Mark McGhee in June 2009.

ABERDEEN MANAGERS' RECORDS

		P	W	D	L
Jimmy Philip	1903-1924	726	263	186	277
Pat Travers	1924-1938	576	271	124	181
Dave Halliday	1938-1955	436	206	76	154
Dave Shaw	1955-1959	196	94	24	78
Tommy Pearson	1959-1965	233	87	57	89
Eddie Turnbull	1965-1971	291	140	58	93
Jim Bonthrone	1971-1975	204	96	50	58
Ally MacLeod	1975-1977	76	33	20	23
Billy McNeill	1977-1978	50	31	11	8
Alex Ferguson	1978-1986	455	271	106	78
Ian Porterfield	1986-1988	89	44	32	13
Alex Smith/Jocky Scott	1988-1992	178	93	44	41
Willie Miller	1992-1995	155	72	50	33
Roy Aitken	1995-1997	123	50	29	44
Alex Miller	1997-1998	42	11	12	19
Paul Hegarty	1998-1999	20	7	2	11
Ebbe Skovdahl	1999-2001	159	55	35	69
Steve Paterson	2001-2004	68	23	13	32
Jimmy Calderwood	2004-2009	224	93	57	74

Manager	P	W	D	L	Win ratio
Billy McNeill	50	31	11	8	73.00%
Alex Ferguson	455	271	106	78	71.21%
Ian Porterfield	89	44	32	13	67.42%
Alex Smith/Jocky Scott	178	93	44	41	64.61%
Willie Miller	155	72	50	33	62.58%
Jim Bonthrone	204	96	50	58	59.31%
Eddie Turnbull	293	140	60	93	58.02%
Pat Travers	576	271	124	181	57.81%
Ally MacLeod	76	33	20	23	56.55%
Dave Halliday	436	206	76	154	55.96%
Dave Shaw	196	94	24	78	54.08%
Jimmy Calderwood	224	93	57	74	53.52%
Roy Aitken	123	50	29	44	52.44%
Tommy Pearson	233	87	57	89	49.57%

Ebbe Skovdahl	159	55	35	69	45.60%
Steve Paterson	68	23	13	32	43.38%
Alex Miller	42	11	12	19	40.48%
Paul Hegarty	20	7	2	11	40.00%

GOTHENBURG GREATS

The Aberdeen squad that won the European Cup Winners' Cup in 1983 were revered some 25 years later as the 'Gothenburg Greats' testimonial was set up to honour the players and manager. The Aberdeen Sports Council inducted the complete squad into the City Sporting Hall of Fame, breaking from the tradition of only honouring local-born sportsmen. On July 12th 2008 a testimonial match was arranged against Manchester United at Pittodrie, as most of the squad took their bow with former manager Alex Ferguson after the game. No less than 14 of the original squad followed their manager into coaching or management.

Gothenburg Greats Appearances and Goals for Aberdeen FC

	Lge	LC	SC	Eur	Tot	Gls
Angus, Ian	84	10	15	11	120	12
Bell, Doug	108	29	21	25	183	14
Black, Eric	115	18	25	22	180	70
Cooper, Neale	133	27	27	33	220	10
Gunn, Bryan	14	4	1	1	20	0
Hewitt, John	240	47	34	43	364	89
Kennedy, Stuart	223	55	29	26	333	9
Leighton, Jim	384	54	48	43	529	0
McGhee, Mark	164	35	20	31	250	98
McLeish, Alex	494	74	69	56	693	30
McMaster, John	205	54	28	28	315	33
Miller, Willie	561	109	66	61	797	32
Rougvie, Doug	179	45	26	28	278	21
Simpson, Neil	205	34	34	37	310	31
Strachan, Gordon	183	46	29	34	292	89
Watson, Andy	99	13	12	12	136	17
Weir, Peter	160	21	19	29	229	38
Total	**3551**	**675**	**503**	**520**	**5249**	**593**

SCOTTISH CUP FINAL CAPTAINS

Four different Aberdeen legends have enjoyed the privilege of being captain in the Dons' seven previous Scottish Cup wins. Aberdeen were never fortunate enough to savour a pre-war cup win; the nearest they came was in 1937. It was some ten years and a world war later in 1947 that Aberdeen won the cup for the first time. Only three players from the 1937 final side were still around in the new red jerseys of Aberdeen: George Johnstone, the keeper who had helped Celtic out during the war; the evergreen Willie Cooper and the uncompromising Frank Dunlop, who had been installed as the Aberdeen captain in their bold new era. Aberdeen won 2-1 in a classic final but while the likes of George Hamilton and Stan Williams took all the plaudits, it was Dunlop who kept an eager Hibernian forward line at bay to see his side through to a first Scottish Cup success. Martin Buchan was a local player from a footballing family as his father had previously played for the Dons. Buchan was so promising that Turnbull thought that he simply had to find a regular place in the side for his young star. That was to come in the form of a 'sweeper' role at Pittodrie and it was a position he was to make his own. Buchan joined Aberdeen from Banks O' Dee in 1965 and his emergence was such that he was appointed Aberdeen captain a month short of his 21st birthday in 1970. It was fairytale stuff as less than two months later Buchan was the captain of the Aberdeen side that humbled Celtic 3-1 at Hampden. At 21, Buchan remains the youngest-ever Scottish Cup-winning captain. Aberdeen continued promoting young, emerging, captains when the enthusiastic Ally MacLeod decided to give the captain's armband to a young Willie Miller in December 1975. It began a period of success that was unprecedented at Pittodrie and after Alex Ferguson joined the club in 1978 it was Miller who was the skipper through the glory period with no less than ten major successes coming to Pittodrie which made Aberdeen a side that was feared throughout Europe. Alex McLeish was a youngster who came through the ranks at Pittodrie and he went on to become the most capped player in Aberdeen's history. It was McLeish who took over in time to lift the 1990 Scottish Cup when Aberdeen defeated Celtic on penalties in a thrilling finale to the season.

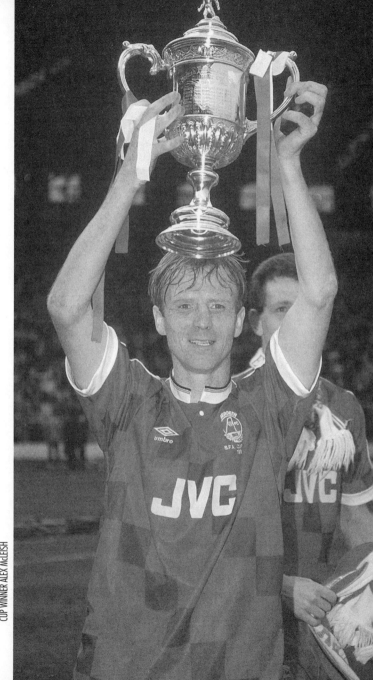

THE DONS OF 1911

Aberdeen came so close to winning the league championship for the first time in 1911, only seven years after they were formed. Despite defeating Rangers home and away before Christmas in the campaign, they eventually lost out to the Ibrox side in a thrilling finish to the season. A 1-0 defeat at Hamilton on March 25th was a hammer blow to Aberdeen who then drew their next three matches to hand Rangers the initiative. With 19 wins from their 34 matches, it was the Dons' best return since their formation. Aberdeen were also the only side that went through the season undefeated at home. Later that year, when Rangers travelled north for a league game, there were chaotic scenes as the visiting players were pelted with stones after some nasty events on the field. The SFA closed Pittodrie for two weeks, but with Aberdeen not due to play again until some weeks later the closure was ineffective.

BEST BETT

Aberdeen manager Alex Ferguson brought midfielder Jim Bett from Lokeren in June 1985 for a £300,000 fee. Jim Bett had enjoyed a somewhat nomadic career up until that point, having started out with Airdrie before moving to Iceland and Valur FC of Reykjavik. Much admired by Belgium boss Guy Thys, Bett returned to Scotland in 1980, as Rangers paid a £150,000 fee for his services. Jim was in the Rangers side that lost to Aberdeen in the 1982 and 1983 cup finals. Bett was included in the squad that went to Italia 1990, and it was a disillusioned Bett that announced his retirement from the international arena following the 1990 competition. He was released by Aberdeen manager Willie Miller in 1994, and returned to Iceland. Jim went on to complete his first-class career with Hearts and Dundee United.

END OF AN ERA

Charlie O'Hagan and Willie Lennie were two Aberdeen legends before the Great War and they played together for the last time in John Edgar's testimonial match in April 1914. Irish international O'Hagan and left winger Lennie struck up a superb partnership at Pittodrie that brought Aberdeen to the semi-finals of the Scottish Cup and a near championship success in 1911.

THE 'BRUSH'

Any Aberdeen player who played for Scotland back in the 1970s would be faced with the long-felt belief that anything parcelled up in a red shirt would have to give that bit extra to gain international recognition. Giving 'extra' epitomised Davie 'The Brush' Robb, the only Dundonian to attain cult status with the Aberdeen support. Robb's erratic flowing locks saw him christened 'Basil Brush' after the infuriating puppet show of the time. Robb was one of a host of Eddie Turnbull signings in the aftermath of the mass Pittodrie exodus of 1965. His arrival as a young hopeful went almost unnoticed as the silky skills of Jimmy Smith drew more attention. In his first-ever senior game he ripped his hometown club Dundee to shreds playing on the right wing in a sensational 5-0 win at Dens Park in a Scottish Cup tie. While he may have been frustrating to watch on occasion, he went on to become an invaluable part of the great Aberdeen side that won the Scottish Cup in 1970. Robb's knack of 'taking the weight off' other Aberdeen strikers made him a perfect foil for the likes of Smith, Harper and Jarvie. While his contribution as a team player was often underestimated, Robb was also well-known by officials throughout his career. His no-nonsense approach to the game often saw him incurring the wrath of officials. In the current climate where a 'Fancy-Dan' approach prevails, Robb had no time for such niceties. In these politically correct times, Davie would probably not last long in the modern game, but back in his time it was far removed from what we see today. Robb's international career was a relatively short one; five caps in 1971 was his lot, he never appeared at Hampden but could add Wembley, Lisbon, Cardiff, Copenhagen and Moscow to his list of destinations. In 1976 Davie came off the bench in the League Cup final to score the winner against Celtic. A year later, his parting shot to the Red Army was a sensational goal against Rangers on Christmas Eve as Aberdeen humbled the Ibrox side in a 4-0 hammering at Pittodrie. It was the end of an era at Pittodrie as Davie was soon off on his travels with the USA his destination. America was never quite ready for Robb although he was immediately christened 'Big Red' by soccer enthusiasts in Tampa. Not many Aberdeen players have had their own songs exclusive to themselves but big Davie's rendition declaring that we didn't need Eusebio summed up the big man in the ultimate one-liner.

DANISH DELIGHT

Aberdeen qualified from the group stages of the Uefa Cup in 2007 after a sensational 4-0 win over Copenhagen at Pittodrie on December 20th. Aberdeen needed to win the game to finish in third place in a tough group. After a goalless first period, the Dons hit the Danish champions with a four-goal salvo in what was another famous European night at Pittodrie. Aberdeen eased through to the last 32 which meant that Lokomotiv Moscow and Copenhagen were eliminated.

QUEEN'S ATTRACT RECORD CROWD

A record attendance of 16,000 filled Pittodrie for the visit of Queen's Park in a Scottish Cup tie on January 28th 1905. In what was Aberdeen's first season in league football, the visit of the famous amateurs was seen as a massive game for Aberdeen and one in which they could showcase themselves in their bid to gain admission to the First Division. Aberdeen defeated the former winners 2-1 with goals from Low and Robertson.

ENCLOSURE NO MORE

One of the better known areas of Pittodrie Park, as it was known, disappeared in the summer of 1968 when the old enclosure at the ground was replaced with new seating. The area in front of the grandstand had been a popular terrace but with new seating extending the stand, it was now named the Main Stand and Pittodrie Park was now called Pittodrie Stadium.

'HOMECOMING'

2009 in Scotland was declared the year of 'Homecoming' as all Scottish people were encouraged to return to their spiritual home. Mark McGhee was certainly in nostalgic mood as he accepted the job as Aberdeen manager in June. The Aberdeen legend from the 1980s declared that it was a bit like a homecoming to Pittodrie and that had great appeal to him. McGhee was Alex Ferguson's first major signing in March 1979 and he went on to become an integral part of the Aberdeen side that was so successful at home and abroad in the 1980s. McGhee left his post at Motherwell and took over as Aberdeen manager from Jimmy Calderwood.

DEANO

Dean Windass was a big signing for the Dons when Roy Aitken paid Hull City £750,000 for the Boothferry Park legend just weeks after the last time Aberdeen won a trophy; the League Cup in 1995. At that time the Dons had recovered from a near-relegation in 1995 to stake a claim at the top again under Aitken. Money seemed no object either as Windass could have been tempted to join a host of clubs in England. It was at Pittodrie that he went on to become a firm favourite in the modern era; his all-action combative style endeared him to the Dons support. Wild goal celebrations and an open dislike for all things Old Firm further warmed supporters to the Englishman. Often seen as fair game by many of Scotland's officials, Windass was certainly one for the big occasion and his never-beaten attitude towards playing was something that has become a rarity these days. Paper talk of the time was full of Dean being touted for a call up to the England squad, with some merit in those claims. Dean, like so many others before him, was never afforded the glare of publicity north of the border from his countrymen. Just like his Aberdeen career had been a rollercoaster of emotion, it all ended in disappointment as Windass was incredibly sent off three times in a game against Dundee United at Tannadice. Such was his passion that it all flared up that day as Roy Aitken was soon shown the exit door at Pittodrie. Dean was soon to follow as a misguided Alex Miller decided to sell Windass to Oxford United for a paltry £400,000 in 1998. The folly of that decision quickly became apparent as Windass was soon on his way to Bradford City in a £1m deal! His career has come full circle as he made a fairytale return to the English Premier with his beloved Hull City in 2008 before becoming player-coach at Darlington.

YOU'RE FIRED!

Aberdeen were never keen to sack managers in the past and it was not until the 1960s that managers were cast aside. Those who have left by 'mutual consent' or have been sacked include; Tommy Pearson, Jim Bonthrone, Ian Porterfield, Alex Smith, Willie Miller, Roy Aitken, Paul Hegarty, Alex Miller, Ebbe Skovdahl, Steve Paterson and Jimmy Calderwood.

THE GREAT WAR

In August 1914 as the Kaiser's troops poured across the border into neutral Belgium, Britain declared war on Germany and immediately looked to enlist 500,000 men for the Army. The Aberdeen contribution to the war effort was admirable during those troubled times. The football club were wholly supportive of the war effort and the club was as shocked as any other to discover that they had to continue to fulfil their fixtures. By the very nature of their geographical position, and the increased activity in the war, those days were without doubt as tough as can be imagined. No less than 14 brave Aberdeen players had joined the armed forces by 1915. Several had been called up while others enlisted to help the war effort. The folly of continuing to play football was highlighted with Aberdeen effectively playing two sides; one for the games at Pittodrie and virtually another to fulfil their away matches. With every resource being put towards the war effort, there was shortage of everything and travelling around the country was ill-advised. Some of the Aberdeen players who lived away from the area found their way to take part in away matches. With crowds dwindling due to the now critical situation in Europe, Aberdeen as a club were effectively surviving from day to day as the likes of Bobby Hannah and Alex Wright were called up to the Army; more would follow as the crisis at home and abroad deepened. The club did consider the prospect of withdrawing from the league as they struggled to meet their commitments. Away from home the club were struggling to get a side together with the influential George Brewster and Jock Wyllie only playing in home matches. It was reported that a club from the west was ready to take Aberdeen's place. If such a development came to fruition, it would have almost certainly meant that Aberdeen would have began life after the war as a non-league club. Such a prospect did not appeal to any of the club members, some of whom were still around from the days of the amalgamation and the struggle to get into the league. Aberdeen continued to survive until almost mercifully football was halted in 1917. No football was played in the area between 1917 and 1919 and Pittodrie closed its doors as the nation braced itself for a long war with no end in sight. League football did not resume until the 1919/20 season.

PAID IN FULL

By December 1920 the plans that were set in place some 17 years previously were rewarded when Aberdeen paid the final instalment due on the purchase of the ground, which meant that Pittodrie was now in the ownership of the club. That allowed the club to push forward plans to build up the embankment on the south side of the ground after paying off the final instalments, with plans to extend the grandstand also in the pipeline. It was a remarkable effort by the club who were facing going out of business during the latter days of the Great War.

TALE OF TWO STANS

With Pittodrie being used for the war effort, football shifted a few hundred yards along the road to nearby Linksfield, owned by the city council. On April 19th 1941, Linksfield played host to a Scotland XI game against the British Army. Stanley Matthews and Stan Mortensen of FA Cup fame both featured as the crowds were thrilled to see such talent during those dark days. Former Aberdeen legend Benny Yorston also played. While Matthews was the best known of the visiting players, it was Mortensen who stole the show with four sensational goals.

ARCHIE KNOX

Archie Knox began his playing career with Forfar Athletic and after spells with St Mirren, Dundee United and Montrose, he embarked on a coaching career that began with his native Forfar. Alex Ferguson brought Knox to Pittodrie as his assistant in 1980 to replace Pat Stanton. Knox was respected as one of the best coaches in the country and was also the Dons' 'European Spy' on many occasions as he would run the rule over Aberdeen opponents. After helping the Dons to enjoy great success, Knox took over as manager in his own right at Dundee in 1983. A short spell back at Pittodrie two years later meant that Knox followed his manager down to Old Trafford in 1986. Archie returned to Scotland to assist Walter Smith at Ibrox before he began his association with the national team. In July 2006 he was appointed Scotland youth supremo and a year later he joined Bolton Wanderers in the English Premiership.

BIG DOUG

Arguably the most lauded cult hero of the 1980s was big Doug Rougvie. The giant defender arrived at Aberdeen as a raw 16-year-old from Dunfermline United in 1972. In those early days there was little to suggest that Rougvie would go on to become as idolised as he did; it was not until 1978 that he would appear in the first team with any frequency. It took a controversial incident in the 1979 League Cup Final against Rangers to propel Rougvie inadvertently into the spotlight. Still seen as relatively inexperienced, the big defender was sent off after a 'clash' with Rangers' Derek Johnstone. While Doug was seen as more of the sinned against than sinner in that game, it did not take long for him to redress that. It was against Rangers at Pittodrie on September 15th 1979 that Rougvie brought about some 'closure' to his previous spat with Johnstone. An all-ticket full house at Pittodrie 'welcomed' Rangers for what was fast becoming the most volatile game in the country. Aberdeen were in irresistible form as they went on to win 3-1. However, when Rougvie came on as a substitute in the second half he almost immediately sent Johnstone spinning in the air with a trademark Rougvie challenge. His retribution was complete when he scored from all of two yards in the 80th minute to complete a miserable afternoon for the visitors. It was in the big clashes that Rougvie excelled; none more so than in the many heated Old Firm encounters that seemed all so frequent back then. Manager Ferguson was adept at his mind games back then and when in Glasgow before any big game he would send the giant figure of Rougvie out for an extended 'warm up'. The Dons defender would take his ranging frame around Parkhead doing a series of exercises right on the touchline and facing the crowd full on. It was classic Ferguson and Rougvie thrived in the heated atmosphere. It was no coincidence that these moves would be repeated in front of the Rangers support at Ibrox. Rougvie, of course, went on to become one of the Gothenburg Greats as he played his part in the Dons side that won the European Cup Winners' Cup in 1983. Almost typically, his Aberdeen career ended after a fall out with Ferguson over a few quid in his pay packet which prompted a move to Chelsea. It just did not look the same to see big Doug in a blue shirt and arguably he was never the same player after leaving Pittodrie in 1984.

DONS EURO BOW

Aberdeen played their first-ever tie in European competition on September 6th 1967 and registered a club-record 10-0 win over KR Reykjavik at Pittodrie in the European Cup Winners' Cup. The Dons' Euro baptism could not have been any easier as they outclassed their amateur rivals. They went on to win the return leg 4-1 but did not escape the wrath of manager Turnbull who said his players were unprofessional in their approach.

THE REDS

In August 1966 the Dons changed to an all-red strip for the first time. The Dons have retained their all-red kit ever since, although they did return to a red shirt and white shorts briefly in 1996. Aberdeen remain the only major Scottish club whose registered first choice colours are red.

BRITAIN'S FIRST £100,000 TEENAGER

The first teenager to be sold for a six-figure sum was Aberdeen's 18-year-old starlet Tommy Craig who joined Sheffield Wednesday in May 1969. Craig had hardly established himself in the Aberdeen side after making his debut against Stirling Albion on December 16th 1967. After just 62 appearances, Craig's potential realised a huge £100,000 fee when he signed for the Owls in June 1969. Jimmy Smith also joined Newcastle at the same time as the two most promising talents at Pittodrie were sold off.

THE NEW BECKENBAUER!

Once described as the 'Next Franz Beckenbauer' young Neale Cooper had gained a big reputation on young shoulders after he signed up with the Dons at the age of 16. Already a schoolboy international, Cooper had to bide his time with the Dons as an emerging central defender. However, it was in midfield that Cooper was to find a regular place in the Aberdeen side. He formed a formidable partnership with Neil Simpson in the Aberdeen 'engine room' and allowed the more subtle skills of Strachan and Weir to flourish. He left Aberdeen in 1986 for Aston Villa when a tribunal set a fee of only £375,000 and returned to Scotland, enjoying brief spells with Rangers and Dunfermline Athletic before embarking on a career in coaching.

DREW ON TARGET

Aberdeen legend Drew Jarvie was a prolific scorer for the Dons during his Pittodrie career after his record £72,000 transfer from Airdrie in 1972. He excelled against some tough European opposition and the Dons striker scored against all six European opponents between 1972 and 1978, including Tottenham Hotspur, Borussia Mönchengladbach, and Molenbeek.

LOSING THE HEAD

One of the most volatile fixtures in Scottish football is any Aberdeen v Rangers meeting. Down the years there have been many classic and controversial clashes, none more so than the game at Ibrox on September 28th 1985. As reigning league champions, Aberdeen were the team to beat. Rangers were certainly up for the battle, but they took things too far after Hugh Burns was sent off for a wild lunge after 30 minutes. From the resultant free kick, Alex McLeish headed past Walker to put Aberdeen ahead. From that point mayhem ensued but Aberdeen held their nerve and the Dons cruised into a 3-0 lead. When Craig Paterson was sent off later in the second half, the Aberdeen players were happy to escape to the safety of the dressing rooms as trouble flared all around the Ibrox stands.

61 AND OUT FOR WILLIE

Aberdeen captain and legend Willie Miller holds the record for the most European appearances for the club with 61. Miller made his European debut against Finn Harps in 1973 and he also scored two goals in European competition; one against Sion in Switzerland in 1982 and one against Gothenburg at Pittodrie in the 1986 European Cup.

MAJESTIC MCDOUGALL

After the Dons had clinched the league championship with three games to spare in 1985, they turned on the style against Hearts at Tynecastle on May 4th 1985 in a 3-0 win that even had the home fans applauding in awe at an Aberdeen side that had shown all of their qualities. Frank McDougall was at his sparkling best and his first-half hat-trick was the end product of some sensational play from the visitors.

WILLIE MILLER'S EURO DEBUT: ABERDEEN IN ACTION AGAINST FINN HARPS

SIMMIE, SIMMIE

Local players making it through to play for their home team has always been a popular trend at Pittodrie. Although born in London, Neil Simpson was brought up in Newmachar and joined Aberdeen in 1978. A product of local youth team Middlefield Wasps, Simmie was a Scotland youth cap before injury to both John McMaster and Gordon Strachan opened the first-team door for Neil in 1980 and he seized the opportunity afforded to him by Alex Ferguson. From that point on, Neil Simpson became a vital part of the Aberdeen side that would go on to unprecedented success at home and abroad. 'Simmie' formed a resolute and youthful partnership alongside Neale Cooper in the Aberdeen engine room that contributed so much to the success Aberdeen achieved during the golden era of the 1980s. As the winners' medals became more frequent, Neil earned the first of his five international caps when he played for Scotland against Northern Ireland at Hampden in 1983, suffering the 'embarrassment' of being replaced by Gordon Strachan in the second half. Simmie reversed the roles a year later when he came on for the 'wee man' against France in Marseilles. Neil's strengths as a player were his commitment and stamina; he was once described by Alex Ferguson as one of the best 'box-to-box' players in Britain. There were also some vital goals along the way; who could forget that memorable night against Bayern Munich when Simpson hammered in to the heart of the German defence before scoring in front of the old Beach End. The goal paved the way for a famous victory in what was Pittodrie's greatest ever night. Later that season, of course, Aberdeen enjoyed their finest hour in Gothenburg and Neil was once asked where he was positioned when John Hewitt headed home that magical winning goal; "Well inside their half" was the response, and what about Cooper? "Don't know, but he would have been well behind me, that's for sure!" That typified the appetite Neil Simpson had for the game and for the club he loved. Neil moved away from Pittodrie and joined Newcastle United in 1989 and after returning to Motherwell for a short spell he came back to the north-east with Cove before retiring. Simmie returned to Pittodrie in 2002 to take up his present role heading up the Dons community coaching initiatives, which were rewarded nationally some years ago with official recognition for his team's efforts by the league sponsors.

HIGHLAND ROUT

Peterhead were on the end of the Dons' record win in 1923 when Aberdeen crushed the Highland League side 13-0 at Pittodrie in a Scottish Cup tie. The original tie was scheduled for Recreation Park in Peterhead but Aberdeen requested that the tie be switched to Pittodrie to attract a bigger crowd. While that was accepted by Peterhead, it was a hugely unpopular decision amongst their players who genuinely believed they had a chance to cause an upset. As it turned out, several Peterhead players didn't play and the Dons went on to create their record victory. The irony was that dreadful weather conditions kept the crowd down to 3,241 which did not bring the expected cash windfall for the part-time club.

PAUL BREITNER

The German World Cup-winner enjoyed a memorable career for club and country, and Pittodrie played a part in that. As an emerging youngster, Breitner was in the German side that played in the 1970 Uefa Youth Championships at Pittodrie. Breitner went on to become a world-class midfielder with Bayern Munich and Germany. However, his last appearance at Aberdeen was with Bayern in the Dons' 3-2 European Cup Winners' Cup quarter-final win in 1983.

PREMIER ELITE

League reconstruction at the end of season 1974/75 meant that the changes in Scottish football were as radical as any previous shake up. A new 10-team 'super league' was introduced with each team playing each other four times a season. Initially, two sides were relegated from the ten, but that was latterly seen as too cut-throat and several changes have since been made. The SPL brand came into force in 1999 and the top division consisted of 12 clubs with the new top six 'split' meaning teams would play 38 league games.

COSMOPOLITAN ABERDEEN

In 2000 Aberdeen were more like a league of nations with no less than seven different nationalities. Aberdeen's first-team pool consisted of players from Scotland, England, Argentina, Morocco, Norway, Bulgaria and Germany.

ABERDEEN IN THE LEAGUE CUP

Ever since winning the inaugural Southern League Cup in 1946, Aberdeen have gone on to win the League Cup on five occasions. After reaching the final in 1947, and the semi-final a year later, the Dons struggled for several years before their first official success in the tournament in 1955. Aberdeen were reigning league champions and were installed as favourites to beat St Mirren in the Hampden final. Aberdeen were the only undefeated team in Britain going into the game and eventually won through 2-1. Aberdeen showed a new found determination to succeed and added the League Cup to the championship title they won some months earlier. It was perhaps an indication of the Dons' rising stock in the game that they went in to the semi-final that year against Rangers as clear favourites... and they did not disappoint. In 1966 Aberdeen reached the semi-final under Eddie Turnbull only to go down to Rangers at Hampden in a replay. In 1976 Aberdeen took the trophy back to Pittodrie for the first time in 21 years. It took an extra-time goal from substitute Davie Robb to give Aberdeen victory after Drew Jarvie had levelled a Kenny Dalglish penalty. It was the first time that Willie Miller had led the Dons to success as he was to embark on a memorable career laden with silverware. In 1985, Alex Ferguson demanded his side win the one trophy that had eluded him in his memorable Pittodrie career and the Dons completed the task in some style by going through all six ties without conceding a single goal. Hibernian were no match for the Dons in the 12-minute final; noted after the Dons hit two goals in the opening period. The Dons' next success came in 1989, against Rangers, to win the tie in extra time. That win was crucial, as the Dons had lost the previous two finals to their arch rivals. In 1995 under Roy Aitken the Dons brought back a glimmer of the good old days by winning the cup against Dundee at Hampden. Goals from Dodds and Shearer took the cup north. Once again the Dons had to see the Old Firm off to succeed and that season it was Rangers and Paul Gascoigne who were put to the sword in the Hampden semi-final. It was a majestic performance from Eoin Jess that saw the Dons midfielder embarking on an extravagant piece of showboating in the closing minutes.

ENTER SIR ALEX

For the third consecutive season, Aberdeen had a new manager in place when Alex Ferguson took over at Pittodrie in the summer of 1978. With Ally MacLeod taking over as Scotland coach, and Billy McNeill being fast-tracked back to Celtic a year later, it was certainly a new era at Aberdeen. Ironically, Ferguson arrived at Aberdeen on the back of an acrimonious parting with St Mirren. The rest, as they say, is history…

STUART KENNEDY

Signed from Falkirk for £25,000 by Ally MacLeod in the summer of 1976, Kennedy was already an under-23 international before he joined the Dons. A tough, tenacious full-back, Kennedy was once described as the "ultimate professional" by Alex Ferguson. A firm favourite at Pittodrie, Kennedy would certainly have gained more than his eight Scotland caps had it not been for the Old Firm pair of Sandy Jardine and Danny McGrain. Kennedy was in the Aberdeen side that won the League Cup in 1976 and he played his part in the Aberdeen success story right up until a cruel injury suffered in the European Cup Winners' Cup semi-final match against Waterschei in Belgium effectively ruled him out of a starting place in Gothenburg. Eventually Kennedy was forced to retire from the game due to injury.

"ONE GOAL AND WE ARE RIGHT BACK IN IT!"

The famous half-time quote from Aberdeen legend Drew Jarvie as Aberdeen contemplated a second half against Liverpool at Anfield in the Champions Cup in 1980. The problem was that a young and weakened Aberdeen side were already 3-0 down to the English champions who would go on to lift the European Cup later that season. Aberdeen eventually went down 4-0 to arguably the best club side ever seen in English football.

ALL DRAWN OUT

In what was an exhaustive 44-game season in 1993/94, under Willie Miller the Dons once again came second behind Rangers. As the goal rush from the previous season failed to materialise, it was a record number of 21 drawn games that proved detrimental in the Dons' attempts to take the title.

BACK FROM THE BRINK AND A CLASSY 'KEEPY UP'

Not unlike the first season of the Premier League in 1976 when Aberdeen were almost relegated yet went on to win the League Cup some months later, their efforts were repeated in 1995, the last occasion the club won a major trophy. Aberdeen just managed to escape a first-ever relegation in May 1995 and saved their status after an historic Premier League play-off success over Dunfermline Athletic. Under Roy Aitken, Aberdeen went on to lift the League Cup in style with a 2-0 win over Dundee at Hampden. On their way to the final, the Dons beat Rangers in the semi-final with two Billy Dodds goals. That game was also remembered for Eoin Jess and his audacious 'keepy-up' routine in the closing moments to rub salt into Rangers' wounds.

HAVE YOU SEEN TZANKO?

In the days when Aberdeen were happy to spend millions in a transfer market that gave little or no return for their investments, arguably the most ludicrous transfer was that of Bulgarian defender Tzanko Tzvetanov. Rumours were that fellow countryman Ilian Kiriakov, who joined Aberdeen for £400,000 and a hefty signing on fee and salary, had recommended his mate to the club. Worse still was the decision to splash out £600,000 on a Bulgarian defender who manager Roy Aitken had never seen play! Not surprisingly, Tzvetanov flattered to deceive along with international buddy Kiriakov who was effectively signed on the back of one promising performance playing for Famagusta against Paul Gascoigne of Rangers in a European Champions Cup qualifying tie.

DONS WIN CUP AND FERGIE'S FURY!

Aberdeen completed a remarkable cup double with another Scottish Cup victory over Rangers in a 1-0 win on May 21st 1983. Coming ten days after Aberdeen had won the European Cup Winners' Cup, it was a frustrating final and it took an Eric Black header in extra time to take the trophy north for the second year in succession. Immediately on full time manager Alex Ferguson was scathing of his players as they fell below the standards that were expected from him. The Aberdeen manager later apologised to his players.

UNCLE EBBE

The strange tale of Danish manager Ebbe Skovdahl, who presided over some of the worst moments in the club's history, yet still managed to escape the wrath of the support. The likeable Dane was the Dons' first foreign coach when appointed in 1999, but a disastrous 5-0 hammering at home to Celtic in his first game was an ominous sign. Six league games later and not a single goal scored – they were tough times for the club. Under Ebbe, the Dons managed to finish adrift at the bottom of the league in his first season with a record 83 goals conceded and an incredible 35 different players used. Two domestic cup final appearances proved futile and Skovdahl eventually left in December 2002, after spending a small fortune and taking Aberdeen to new levels of mediocrity.

MILLER MAKING PLANS FOR NIGEL

Alex Miller may well have enjoyed a successful time in his supporting role at Liverpool in recent years, but he was an unqualified disaster when in charge at Aberdeen. After managing to keep the club away from relegation trouble in 1998, hopes were high that the team at least would progress under the former Hibernian manager. However, eleven games without a win in 1998/99 brought an abrupt end to Miller's tenure. It was an alarming, carefree approach to the transfer dealings that did not help; the most glaring of which was the £300,000 wasted on Nigel Pepper, brought in from English football.

IT'S NAE REAL!

Real Madrid – the famous Spanish giants who were humbled by Aberdeen in the final of the 1983 European Cup Winners' Cup in Sweden – were the original masters in the early days of European football, winning the first five European Cups. With the legendary Alfredo Di Stefano at the helm, they were firm favourites to see off the Aberdeen challenge, a team that was competing in their first European final. Two hours of Gothenburg rain and it was Aberdeen who prevailed in a 2-1 win that had the great Di Stefano full of praise for the Scots; "Aberdeen have what money can't buy; a soul, a team spirit built on a family tradition."

NINE IN A ROW

The sequence represents the longest winning run Aberdeen enjoyed in European football between August 1982 and April 1983. As Aberdeen went on to win the European Cup Winners' Cup that season, their only defeat was a 1-0 reverse in Belgium against Waterschei. Aberdeen had won the first leg 5-1 at Pittodrie. Aberdeen's longest unbeaten run was ten matches between August 1982 and April 1984, when Porto knocked Aberdeen out of the ECWC at the semi-final stage. The Dons were attempting to become the first team to retain the trophy.

JIMMY PHILIP

Jimmy Philip stood down as manager in July 1924 as former player Pat Travers replaced him as Aberdeen manager. Trainer Peter Simpson had previously retired to make way for Billy Russell, and it was thought that this had a bearing on Philip's decision to step down. Philip was the first Aberdeen manager in 1903 and he was one of the main reasons Aberdeen were admitted to the Scottish League a year later. Philip was never afraid to champion the Aberdeen cause and was forthright in his views, which often landed him in trouble with the authorities. Right up until his last days in charge at the club, he was not against bending the rules as he was reported for 'tapping' a Richmond Junior player in Aberdeen. Philip became a club director but a road accident in Belfast on July 11th 1930 led to his untimely passing.

NO PAIN NO GAIN IN CUP

Lowly Clydebank came north to Pittodrie for a Scottish Cup match on February 11th 1970. The midweek tie had an almost surreal atmosphere as Aberdeen were playing in an unfamiliar blue and white striped kit, hurriedly secured from a local junior club after the Bankies turned up with their familiar red diagonal strip. It was also the first game as captain for a young Martin Buchan. The ingredients were in place for a cup shock and for long periods the visitors more than matched an Aberdeen side that struggled to gain supremacy. A narrow 2-1 win saw the Dons players roundly jeered at full time. Exactly two months later, Martin Buchan led Aberdeen to cup glory with a 3-1 win over Celtic at Hampden in the final.

BIG ECK

Alex McLeish was given the moniker by the Aberdeen supporters. McLeish arrived at Aberdeen from Glasgow United in 1976, and was brought through the ranks at Pittodrie and made his debut for the Dons in January 1978 under Billy McNeill. Often deployed in a midfield role in his early days at the club, it was his partnership with Willie Miller at the heart of the Aberdeen defence that laid the foundations for such prolonged success. Alex went on to graduate from the Scotland under-21 side to become the Dons' most capped player with 77 appearances. McLeish also had the distinction of being captain on eight occasions. It was Alex McLeish who scored a sensational equaliser against Rangers in the 1982 Scottish Cup Final that paved the way for future success. After enjoying success at home and in Europe with Aberdeen, McLeish took over as Aberdeen captain in 1990 from Miller and eventually left the club four years later to take up a coaching role with Motherwell. After spells with Hibernian and Rangers, McLeish took over as Scotland coach and nearly took the country to the European Championship finals in Austria and Switzerland in 2008. McLeish left his post with the SFA after the end of their qualifying campaign and took over as manager at Birmingham City.

"LIKE SHOOTING DUCKS AT THE FAIR"...

...was Aberdeen manager Alex Smith's reaction to the Dons' dramatic Scottish Cup penalty shoot-out against Celtic in the final of 1990. It was the first occasion that the cup final had been settled in this way, and the last time that Aberdeen won the trophy. Theo Snelders saved Celtic's Anton Rogan's penalty, which left the way clear for Brian Irvine to create his own piece of history by scoring the decisive spot kick. The Dons won 9-8.

OPTING OUT

The local Aberdeenshire Cup may be one of the oldest in Scottish football, and the magnificent trophy has certainly taken pride of place in the Aberdeen boardroom on no less than 38 occasions. However, Aberdeen opted out of the competition in 1934 and did not return until 1980. Since then, the club have put forward their youth and reserve sides to compete for the cup which is played for by the local regional clubs from the Highland League.

500 NOT OUT IN LEAGUE CUP

John McMaster had the distinction of scoring Aberdeen's 500th goal in the League Cup when he scored against Meadowbank Thistle on August 29th 1979. Other notable landmarks in the League Cup were Scott Booth scoring the Dons' 700th in the competition against St Mirren in 1995. Aberdeen went on to win the trophy that year. The 100th goal was scored by 1950s legend Harry Yorston against Rangers at Ibrox in 1951.

FIRST EURO DEFEAT

Aberdeen lost 3-2 to Borussia Mönchengladbach at Pittodrie on September 13th 1972 in what was the Dons' first-ever defeat in a home tie in European football after a run of seven opponents which included Standard Liege, Juventus and Celta Vigo. Following Molenbeek in 1977 and Liverpool in 1980, the Dons did not lose at home until Porto won at Pittodrie in the second leg of the 1984 European Cup Winners' Cup competition.

SCORING FOR FUN

Aberdeen went an incredible 33 consecutive Scottish Cup ties between 1937 and 1951 scoring in every game. The sequence began with a 6-0 win over Highland League side Inverness Thistle at Pittodrie on January 30th 1937, and finished with a 4-0 win over Third Lanark in 1951. Aberdeen travelled to Celtic Park in the next round and went down 3-0. Included in that run were the 1937 and 1947 finals against Celtic and Hibernian, and an 8-0 win over Ayr United in February 1947.

FOURS UP

Legends George Hamilton and Joe Harper both have the distinction of scoring four goals for Aberdeen in League Cup ties on two occasions. 'Gentleman' George scored four in the Dons' first-ever League Cup group game against Falkirk in September 1946. Hamilton repeated that feat with four against Queen of the South a year later as Aberdeen went on to reach the final. Joe Harper scored four against Airdrie in a 7-3 win at Pittodrie on August 22nd 1970. In his second spell with the Dons, Harper scored four against Hamilton Academical in October 1978 in a second leg tie.

LOCAL HERO

John Hewitt came through the ranks as a young player at Pittodrie and went on to become part of Aberdeen FC history when he scored the winning goal that took the European Cup Winners' Cup to Aberdeen in 1983. Being a local player the occasion was all the more special although Hewitt became known as a 'super-sub' such was his impact when he would come on. Hewitt went on to score many vital goals for the club during that golden age, including a record 9.6-second winner against Motherwell in the Scottish Cup in 1982. That goal set up Aberdeen for success that year and qualification for the European Cup Winners' Cup. Hewitt was also on the mark in the 1985 and 1986 cup finals against Hibernian and Hearts. He went on to make 364 appearances for the Dons, scoring 89 goals.

WEMBLEY WIZARD

Alex Jackson was spotted playing in 1924 in America by former Don Jock Hume, who recommended Jackson to Aberdeen. His one full season at Pittodrie was a memorable one and it was after that when Huddersfield Town paid a record £5,000 to take Jackson to England. Jackson was part of the Scotland side that was christened the 'Wembley Wizards' after a crushing 5-1 win over England in 1928. Jackson scored three of the Scotland goals. He would later join Chelsea and later in his career he moved to France with Nice. It was while serving with the Army in Egypt in 1946 that Jackson was tragically killed in a road accident.

FABULOUS FRANK

After Mark McGhee left Aberdeen to join SV Hamburg in 1984, manager Alex Ferguson moved swiftly to replace him with St Mirren striker Frank McDougall. The former Clydebank striker had been around for several years but it was when he joined Aberdeen in a £100,000 deal that he embarked on a scoring spree with his new club. Included in his two seasons with the club was a four-goal blitz of Celtic and a crucial winner against Servette in the 1986 European Cup. McDougall was part of the last Aberdeen side that won the league title in 1985 and was also a league and Scottish Cup winner in 1985/86. He played 70 games for the Dons, scoring 44 goals, before a back injury forced an early retirement.

JOHNNY MAC

Widely regarded as the best uncapped player ever at Pittodrie, John McMaster was another Aberdeen player who played a huge role in the Dons' success in the 1980s. McMaster joined the club from Port Glasgow in 1971, another Bobby Calder find that was persuaded to come north. McMaster made his mark under Ally MacLeod but it was not until Alex Ferguson switched him to a deeper midfield and defensive role that McMaster became a regular in the side. He was on the verge of full international honours in 1980 when he was badly injured against Liverpool in a European Cup tie at Pittodrie which sidelined him for 18 months. McMaster came back and played his part in the Dons' 1983 European Cup Winners' Cup success. In 1985 he received a testimonial from the club and two years later returned to his native Greenock and played for Morton.

100 EUROS

German side Hertha Berlin provided the opposition for what was Aberdeen's 100th match in European football when the sides met at Pittodrie on September 17th 2002 in a Uefa Cup tie. Aberdeen battled out a 0-0 draw before going down 1-0 in the Berlin return.

BURNING EMBERS

In the days before Pittodrie the original Aberdeen played out of the tight and atmospheric surroundings of the Chanonry and on one occasion after a game, the fire in the hut that served as a changing room went out. One of the Aberdeen players went to search for firewood in the adjacent grounds but was spotted by the master of the house who promptly invited the team back to his home for an after-match talk, the local resident being a keen supporter.

FIRST ENGLISHMAN

The original Aberdeen FC supplied the first-ever English-born professional for a Scottish league match when Wilf Toman had a trial for Dundee as they took on Rangers at Ibrox in March 1896. Toman was a regular in the Aberdeen side that was playing in the Northern League and not yet part of the Scottish top flight.

JOCK HUTTON

The burly defender made his name as a tough, uncompromising full-back with a fierce shot during his spell at Aberdeen in the early 1920s. In the aftermath of the Great War, Hutton became one of the great personalities at the time. Signed as a centre forward it was as a defender that he excelled. He went on to become the club's most capped player at that time. On April 30th 1924, Hutton received a benefit match from Aberdeen as they welcomed Liverpool – the English league champions of 1922 and 1923 – to Pittodrie for a first visit to Aberdeen. A good crowd of around 6,000 turned out to see the teams draw 1-1. In October 1926 Jock Hutton was sold for a record £5,000 to Blackburn Rovers. In 1928 he played for Rovers in the FA Cup final against Huddersfield Town before a 92,041 crowd, in direct opposition to former teammate Alec Jackson who scored Huddersfield's only goal in a game that finished in a 3-1 win for Blackburn.

WEIR MAGIC

Uefa Cup holders Ipswich Town were expected to see off the considerable challenge of Aberdeen when the sides were paired in the 1981 competition. Ipswich had just won the trophy some three months earlier and the English media were happy to put Aberdeen down as fodder against a side that was expected to make a serious challenge for the English league. With Bobby Robson in charge and a wealth of international talent at their disposal, Aberdeen were rank outsiders after a shaky start to their own campaign. The odds shifted slightly after an impressive Dons side came away from the first leg in Suffolk with a 1-1 draw. The Dons fell behind through a Thijssen strike before John Hewitt levelled the tie in the second half. This set up an enthralling return tie at Pittodrie on September 30th 1981. Ipswich boss Robson claimed that Aberdeen "could not play as well as that again" after the first game. A capacity, fevered crowd at Pittodrie saw the Dons eventually sweep aside the holders in a whirlwind second half. Two goals from Peter Weir proved crucial as Aberdeen went on to win 3-1 in what was one of those special European nights at the old stadium. Peter Weir still works for the club as chief scout in the west of Scotland.

MANCHESTER UNITED, JUVENTUS, PORTO & ABERDEEN!

Not a set of teams lined up on a games console but actually the last four clubs that reached the semi-final stages of the 1984 European Cup Winners' Cup competition. As cup holders, Aberdeen were actually the bookies' favourites to retain the cup, even in such exalted company. British football followers were expecting a dream final between Aberdeen and Manchester United in Switzerland, but it was not to be as both were knocked out at the semi-final stage. Aberdeen were disappointing as they went down to an emerging Porto side, losing both ties 1-0. Some years later it emerged that Romanian referee Igna was the subject of a bribery scandal.

SHUT OUT KING

Jim Leighton remains the most-capped keeper in Scottish football history. In between his two spells with the Dons, Leighton went a remarkable ten consecutive internationals without conceding a goal between 1990 and 1997. Since the defeat by Brazil in the 1990 World Cup, Leighton helped Scotland reach France 1998 and kept clean sheets against Sweden (two), San Marino (two), Estonia, Austria, Finland, Greece, the Faroes and Russia. In his 91 games for his country, Jim kept 45 clean sheets, another Scottish record.

ABERDEEN 0-10 SCOTLAND

International football came to Aberdeen on June 1st 1889 as the Scotland side took on Aberdeen at the Chanonry. Some ten years before the club was to move to Pittodrie the old ground was full as a first glimpse of international stars attracted widespread attention in the area. Scotland had just defeated England 3-2 at the Kennington Oval and only three players were missing from that side – and they turned on the style in a comfortable 10-0 win.

CUP FEVER

Between February and April 1947, Aberdeen played a remarkable ten cup ties in succession with no league games. As Aberdeen had made progress in both the Scottish and League Cups, some replayed matches meant that Aberdeen had to shelve their league season while they went on to win the Scottish Cup at Hampden after losing the final of the League Cup to Rangers.

JOHAN CRUYFF

In 1983, after the legendary Johan Cruyff was in Scotland playing in a friendly against Rangers at Ibrox, the Dutchman said at the post-match press conference when asked about Scottish football; "Aberdeen are a side feared across Europe, no doubt about that. I have played against Celtic, Rangers and St Mirren in the last 18 months and I have the greatest respect for Scottish football. It has a style all of its own and I have noticed that Aberdeen have taken over as the top club side in Scotland. Given the traditional strength of Rangers and Celtic that is some achievement. We have all known about Aberdeen for some time and the fact that they have now combined a tactical awareness to go with their commitment. It makes for a potent combination and Aberdeen have that in abundance."

ENGLISH AMATEURS NO MATCH FOR ABERDEEN

English amateur side West Norwood visited Pittodrie in 1906 in what was a friendly that failed to rise above the mediocre; Aberdeen were by far the more experienced side and ran out 4-2 winners in a match that was played in dreadful weather conditions. The team from central London, 'The Bantams' offered stubborn resistance but goals from Henry Low, Charlie Mackie (2) and Scottish international of the future Willie Lennie, secured victory for Aberdeen.

BATTLE OF THE DONS IN IRVINE'S BIG NIGHT

In what was a novel idea, the battle of the English and Scottish Dons came about in Brian Irvine's testimonial on March 28th 1997. Irvine was one of the most popular defenders ever to grace Pittodrie and his testimonial against Wimbledon was a fitting tribute to a memorable Pittodrie career. Irvine scored the all-important penalty that won the Scottish Cup for the Dons in 1990, and also played on nine occasions for his country. Wimbledon were enjoying their best-ever season in the English Premiership, and were sitting in third place in the league when they arrived at Pittodrie. In what was a very entertaining game, Duncan Shearer scored the Dons goal in a 1-1 draw. ABERDEEN: Stillie, Telfer, Tzvetanov, Rowson, Irvine, Inglis, Koumbouare, Craig, Windass, Shearer, Glass. Subs: Whelan, Woodthorpe, Anderson, Buchan, Booth.

BURSTING AT THE SEAMS

"Walking down the Merkland Road" is a legendary line in a famous Aberdeen song which has been aired by generations of Aberdeen supporters. Back in the 1930s it was not so much a walk as a crawl; quite often the thronging crowds would come to a standstill as the main point of entry into Pittodrie was through the granite façade that still exists at the bottom of Merkland Road. The Main Stand, or 'grandstand' as it was known, was usually the only part of the ground that was made all-ticket. Back in 1908 a record 20,000 crowd filled Pittodrie for the visit of Celtic in the Scottish Cup semi-final. As the ground was developed further in the 1920s the capacity of Pittodrie increased dramatically. There was no crowd limit in those days. Supporters were 'guided' through to the ground by stewards and it was more a 'rack em and stack em' attitude. Youngsters would be allowed down to the front so they could see the action. It was not unusual to see the young ones sitting, kneeling and standing, forming a three-tier line. In March 1935 it was another visit from Celtic on Scottish Cup duty that attracted a 40,105 crowd to Pittodrie. In the days of the famous Black & Golds, it was Willie Mills and Matt Armstrong that thrilled the huge crowd in a 3-1 win. The cup always held that special appeal and for years success in the cup was viewed as more important than any league success. As a provincial club Aberdeen invariably had more of a chance in the Scottish Cup and coming up against the Old Firm and the Edinburgh clubs always brought out huge crowds. The club record attendance came in 1954 with the visit of Hearts in the fourth round. When the draw was made the club decided not to make the ground all-ticket but such was the interest in the game that decision was reversed. The official gate of 45,061 still stands but there has been some doubt that the record was not beaten a year later. When Rangers came north in a sixth round tie the attendance was given as 44,647. It emerged some time later that figure did not include season ticket holders which at that time amounted to nearly 900. As there is no record of that total not being included for the Hearts crowd a year earlier, there remains some doubt as to the largest-ever crowd to gather at Pittodrie.

KEEPING YOUR HAND IN

Former Dons full-back Jock Hume kept his 'hand' in after hanging up his boots at Pittodrie in 1921. Hume emigrated to the States and took up a new line of work in Brooklyn, New York, as a masseur. Jock was responsible for spotting some talent over in the USA and among those that came under his critical eye was a young Alec Jackson.

DNIPRO DRAW FIRST FOR DONS

After a tough 0-0 draw against Ukrainian side Dnipro in a first round Uefa Cup tie in 2007 at Pittodrie, Aberdeen created their own piece of club history when they held the Ukraine side to a 1-1 draw in the return leg. Darren Mackie's goal ensured Aberdeen would go through to the group stages of the Uefa Cup for the first time and it was also the first occasion that Aberdeen progressed in a European tie by the away goals method. It was widely regarded as the £1m goal as further involvement in the competition was assured. Previously, Aberdeen had fallen to Gothenburg in 1986, Feyenoord (1987), Rapid Vienna (1989), Skonto Riga (1994) and Bohemians in 2000, by the away goals rule.

TAKE IT AS RED

Aberdeen first wore red shirts on March 18th 1939 in a league game against Queen's Park at Pittodrie. The club were changing from the black and gold strip that had been used since 1904. No reason was given for the change other than only Third Lanark in Scotland sported red and Aberdeen were keen to move away from their traditional black and gold strips that had been synonymous with the club for many years. Aberdeen have since retained red as their primary colours and they remain the only top side in Scotland with a red strip.

CRESCENT CRICKET CLUB

When Pittodrie was first opened in 1899, football and cricket was played at the ground. The Crescent Cricket Club still held a lease on the ground at that time. Aberdeen FC were keen to become sole tenants as they had began paying off the loan and also had long-term plans for expanding the ground.

ABERDEEN TAKE TO THE FIELD ON A MEMORABLE NIGHT IN UKRAINE

LIVERPOOL LESSON FOR DONS

As Scottish League champions, Aberdeen entered the European Cup for the first time in 1980. In those pre-Champions League days, Europe's most coveted tournament was still played on a knockout basis although the elite clubs were seeded in the first round. Aberdeen had still to reach such lofty heights and in comparison to Liverpool, they were strictly novices in the European arena. The Dons had emerged from a tough initial tie against Austria Memphis and their no-scoring draw in Vienna was perhaps their greatest result on foreign soil to date. Liverpool manager Bob Paisley expected a tough time against the Scots. His regret was that one of the two British representatives in the European Cup would be eliminated so early in the tournament. If Aberdeen were looking for encouragement before the tie, then it came in Liverpool's recent form in Europe. In the past two seasons Nottingham Forest and Dynamo Tbilisi had knocked them out in early rounds. However, the Anfield giants posted their intent in the first round by hitting hapless Finnish side Palloseura in a 10-0 win. There was unprecedented demand and interest as the media immediately classed the game as the 'Battle of Britain'. This title was appropriate given the current stature of both clubs in their domestic leagues. The game kicked off in a frenzied atmosphere with around 500 Liverpool fans huddled in the far corner of the Main Stand. Aberdeen had never adopted a cavalier approach at home against the quality of a team like Liverpool but fate dealt the Dons a cruel card after only five minutes when Liverpool scored. John McMaster had been off the field receiving treatment and it was then that the visitors hit Aberdeen with a sucker punch. Terry McDermott drifted over to the Dons right and clipped the ball over Jim Leighton to give the Anfield side a crucial away goal. There was further dismay for the Dons when they lost McMaster shortly after when he was on the end of a brutal challenge from Ray Kennedy. The influential Dons midfielder took no further part and he was to be out of the game with a cruciate injury for more than a year. Aberdeen never really recovered although they had to press Liverpool in search of a goal. It was that early goal that changed the Dons' whole approach as Alex Ferguson stated afterwards that he could not afford to commit his players forward as that would have played in to Liverpool's hands.

BROAD STREET BLUES

Police had to be called to keep order outside the old Journal's offices in Broad Street in February 1908. The reason for their action was down to the 'amazing scenes' as the huge crowd got word of an Aberdeen goal in a replayed Scottish Cup tie against Dundee. Pandemonium ensued as Aberdeen's Willie Lennie scored for the Black & Golds.

NO BOHEMIAN RHAPSODY FOR DONS

Not many sides finish bottom of their respective league and yet still qualify for European football. In 2000 Aberdeen ended up with the SPL wooden spoon but went through to the Uefa Cup on the back of the Fair Play spot that went to Scotland. After a four-year absence from European football it was a young Aberdeen side that went down 2-1 in the first leg against Bohemians in what was one of the Dons' most shameful nights in Europe. Despite dominating the game for long spells it was a late double blow that consigned Aberdeen to a first leg defeat and left themselves with it all to do in the return. Robbie Winters appeared to have given the Dons victory when he scored midway through the second half, but some sloppy defending late in the match proved disastrous for the Dons. With just eight minutes left a Molloy corner was met by the unmarked Sean Maher who headed past Ryan Esson. Then in the last minute, Mark Perry inexplicably tripped O'Keefe in the box and Molloy scored with the penalty. That sent the small band of Irish supporters into raptures. It was a humiliation for the Dons and that feeling was compounded by the Irish celebrations. It seemed that Aberdeen manager Skovdahl had no answer and was left to lick his wounds and face the subsequent flak that would no doubt come his way in the media. Despite winning the return leg 1-0 in Ireland, Aberdeen went out on away goals.

DUTCH DELIGHT

Scotland played Holland at Pittodrie in a European Youth Championship tie in 1980. Included in the Dutch side were Ruud Gullit and Ronald Koeman. Aberdeen had three youngsters in the Scotland squad with Neale Cooper, Neil Simpson and John Hewitt all featuring in the game.

MCKIMMIE MAGIC

Former Dons captain and Scotland international Stewart McKimmie was never a renowned scorer for the Dons but his first senior goal for Aberdeen was certainly an important one. The Aberdeen and Scotland international full-back was the Dons hero on May 2nd 1985. He scored the only goal of the game at Tynecastle to clinch the Premier League title for the Dons.

DON'T DALLY

Dally Duncan became the first Aberdonian to play for Scotland at Pittodrie when he scored in the Scots' 3-2 win over Wales in 1934. Duncan never played for his hometown club and spent most of his career in England with Derby County. Duncan joined Hull City from Aberdeen Junior club Richmond in 1928. Duncan joined Derby County in a £2,000 transfer in 1932 where he spent 14 seasons with the Rams.

DOES GO NAP AGAINST GERS

Not since the Premier League began in 1975 had Aberdeen been such convincing winners over Rangers with a thumping 5-1 win in January 1985. This record win over the Gers was a personal triumph for Frank McDougall, who weighed in with an impressive hat-trick. On a frosty surface it was the Aberdeen players who were the more fleet of foot and were ahead in every department. As league champions the Dons looked imperious at times, spearheaded by the dashing McDougall. The Dons hitman struck twice in the opening 15 minutes to send the Dons fans wild with delight, gorging themselves in glory as McDougall celebrated his goals in style. Rangers tried to hold it all together but looked well out of sorts at the back. Nicky Walker was a busy man and had it not been for some fine saves from him the final result could have been far more embarrassing for the Gers. Tom McQueen rounded off a fine day for the Dons by hitting an 82nd-minute penalty high into the top corner. Rangers' solitary goal from Robert Prytz was nothing more than token defiance. Aberdeen moved eight points clear of Celtic as another title was soon on its way to Pittodrie. The only dark moment for the Dons was the sending off, just before half-time, of Stewart McKimmie and Ally Dawson.

KEEPER CLARK WAS DREAMING

From Premier League strugglers, to a side that was capable of wrecking the Old Firm monopoly in Scottish football in the space of twelve months, was exactly what former Aberdeen boss Ally MacLeod achieved in 1976 after he took over at Pittodrie. The manager danced a jig of delight down the Hampden touchline as he watched his players take Rangers apart in the semi-final. With Celtic to face in the final, Aberdeen had defeated the Parkhead side only two weeks previously to go top of the table and never before had the Dons entered a final so confident of victory. After 12 minutes Dalglish went down tamely after a clash with Jarvie in the box. Referee Paterson decided that the infringement was bad enough to award a penalty but the exchange of words between Jarvie and Dalglish suggested otherwise. The Celtic striker slotted home the penalty to give his side the lead. Aberdeen responded in typical fashion. Arthur Graham had been inspirational on the flanks and enjoyed the wide-open spaces of Hampden to get in behind the Celtic defence. It was another probing run from the Dons winger that set up a goal for Drew Jarvie. Graham crossed to the far post where Joe Harper delightfully set up Jarvie who headed past Latchford. It was no more than Aberdeen deserved and set up a rousing second half. Celtic seemed to be knocked out of their usual fluent stride by an Aberdeen side that kept possession for long periods. Two minutes in to extra time the game settled with a winning goal from Aberdeen substitute Davie Robb. Once again it was Graham who did the spadework and his diagonal run across the Celtic defence set up Harper. The Dons striker passed to Dave Robb who blasted home from close range. It was a goal that triggered a real nervous finale. Celtic threw everything at the Dons but they came up against a defence that had proved so resolute throughout the tournament. Aberdeen keeper Bobby Clark revealed after the game that he had dreamt the night before that Davie Robb would come off the bench and score the winning goal; "I told Davie on the morning of the match and he just grinned. When I saw Davie come on for the extra time period I just knew he was going to do it. He took all of two minutes to make my dream come true though!" claimed Clark after the game.

PLAYING FOR KEEPS

Former Aberdeen keepers Andy Greig and Bobby Clark also played for the club in outfield positions. Clark turned out in a centre-half role after losing his keeper's position to Ernie McGarr in 1969 while Greig also doubled up as a useful right half. Other Aberdeen keepers who have had brief moments in similar roles are Noel Ward and Bryan Gunn.

EIGHTSOME REEL

Aberdeen forward George Ritchie set a club record when he scored eight goals against Aberdeen University in a District League match in 1924. Although the game was not a recognised first team match, it was still officially classed as a competitive fixture.

JUST THE TICKET

When Aberdeen came up against Liverpool in the 1980 European Champions Cup, the news sparked an unprecedented demand for tickets. The club decided to sell their tickets on the morning of a Kilmarnock match at Pittodrie and the scenes down Merkland Road were quite incredible. Many fans queued overnight in freezing temperatures and the whole allocation was sold within 45 minutes. The club was heavily criticised for allowing four tickets per person and many loyal fans were to miss out. It was on the back of this debacle that the club introduced a voucher scheme which has served them and their loyal support well ever since.

FOUR NATIONS AT PITTODRIE

Pittodrie hosted the Four Nations tournament in June 1982 as teams from Scotland, England, Holland and Italy competed. The tournament was open to players from outside the top league in their respective countries. Included in the Scotland side was Bobby Connor of Ayr United, who went on to join Aberdeen from Dundee in 1986 and play for Scotland at full international level. Connor excelled in the tournament and it was on the back of his performances that he earned a transfer to Dundee who were in the top league back then. Tom McQueen of Clyde was also in the Scots side and he found his way to Pittodrie in 1984 as a replacement for Doug Rougvie.

JIMMY MITCHELL, THE PRIDE OF 1955

It was in April 2003 that eight of the 1955 Aberdeen side came from all over the country to visit Pittodrie for a special reunion as guests of the club for the day. Among the players that made the trip was Jimmy Mitchell, the Aberdeen captain from the team that took the first-ever league title to Pittodrie. In the days when huge crowds would not be the sole domain of the Old Firm, Aberdeen regularly played host to massive crowds at Pittodrie and the team in 1955 were indeed a special breed; representing the club was a privilege that they never lost sight of. Jimmy Mitchell arrived at Pittodrie in July 1952 after manager Dave Halliday was keen to sign someone who could lead his emerging side. His £10,000 transfer from Morton was a huge one in those days and Halliday's first task was to make Jimmy team captain. Jimmy made his first team debut along with Paddy Buckley against Motherwell at Fir Park in a League Cup tie on August 9th 1952. Despite a disappointing season in the league Aberdeen made their way through to the Scottish Cup final where they eventually went down to Rangers in a replay. A year later Aberdeen lost to Celtic in the final but it was against arch-rivals Rangers in the semi-final that Mitchell excelled; a crushing, record 6-0 defeat over Rangers remains the Ibrox club's most humiliating defeat in the Scottish Cup. A year later success finally came with the league title coming north. Not only did they have to combat the doubters amongst the Pittodrie crowd; there was never any favourable impressions coming from the south. It made their league championship success all the more worthy. By the time Jimmy Mitchell led his side on to Shawfield on April 9th 1955 little did he know that he was taking Aberdeen on to new and greater heights. It was just another game and a job had to be done. Ninety minutes later Aberdeen were champions and history was made. After Jimmy had led Aberdeen to League Cup success at Hampden in October 1955 he was away to Edinburgh Castle for a television interview. As captain, Jimmy took it upon himself to invite all Aberdonians to welcome the team home at Aberdeen Joint Station that night. Little did Jimmy know but more than 15,000 joyous Aberdeen citizens took him up on his offer. Jimmy was carried shoulder high through the thronging crowds on the team's return.

BIG SIX FOR BIG ECK

Alex McLeish has played in more Scottish Cup finals than any other Aberdeen player. McLeish played in six finals for the Dons, and was only on the losing side on one occasion, in 1993. The Dons legend was captain in 1990 and 1993, and he scored a memorable goal in the 1982 final against Rangers when his curled effort from the edge of the box set the Dons up for a 4-1 win over their Ibrox rivals.

HELLO PELE!

Scotland lost out to Saudi Arabia in the final of the Fifa Under-16 World Cup in 1989 when the tournament was held in Scotland. Pittodrie was the venue for sectional games for East Germany, Australia and Brazil. Scotland also defeated East Germany in the quarter-final of the competition at the Dons ground. During the tournament the great Brazilian legend Pele was with the young Brazilian squad and he did a tour of all of the stadiums; Pele was welcomed with open arms at Pittodrie in what was his first visit to Aberdeen.

SCOTLAND'S SECOND HOME

The Scotland-England under-23 fixture, due at Pittodrie in February 1971, was switched to Hampden Park because of the extensive damaged caused by a fire at the stadium which destroyed part of the Main Stand. The SFA promised Aberdeen that they would host a high profile international fixture by way of compensation, and they delivered on that promise by taking the Scotland v Belgium international to Aberdeen later that year, the first full international away from Hampden for 35 years. John O'Hare scored the only goal of the game in the European Championship qualifying tie.

40,000 AT PITTODRIE

The first attendance in excess of 40,000 at Pittodrie was for a fourth round Scottish Cup tie against Celtic in 1935. A then club record attendance of 40,105 packed Pittodrie as the Black & Golds won 3-1 with goals from Matt Armstrong (2) and Willie Mills. It was also a first-ever Scottish Cup win for Aberdeen over Celtic.

TAKING ON THE 'OLD LADY' OF ITALY

Following their impressive win over Celta Vigo in the first round of the 1971 Uefa Cup, Aberdeen were paired with Italian giants Juventus. Before the first leg there was controversy. With Aberdeen due to play in Turin, neighbours Torino were scheduled to play Austria Vienna on the same night. As Torino's tie was in the Cup Winners' Cup, it took priority over the Dons' Uefa Cup meeting, so the Aberdeen v Juventus game would have to be switched. Initially, Uefa decided that the first leg should now go to Pittodrie, but Aberdeen were against that idea, as any advantage of playing the first leg away would be lost. Uefa agreed that if both teams could agree a suitable alternative date, then the tie could go ahead in Turin. Despite the Dons offering three possible dates, Juventus turned them all down. It was not until the SFA stepped in on Aberdeen's behalf that the game would indeed go ahead in Turin on October 27th 1971. The drawn out saga had strained relations between the clubs and the Dons received a snub from their hosts as no Italian officials were at the airport or hotel to meet the Dons on their arrival in Turin. Without doubt, this was the Dons' toughest test to date in Europe. In the Juve ranks was Pietro Anastasi, the world's most expensive player at £440,000. The Sicilian proved his class after only five minutes when he went past Willie Young to send a swerving shot past Bobby Clark to give the Italians an early lead. From that point on the Dons were under siege, and although outplayed for long spells, they held out until half-time only one goal behind. Aberdeen looked more settled in the second half, and in their first real chance George Murray shot narrowly past. Disaster struck on 55 minutes after the Scots had again weathered the Italian storm. Following a free kick from the edge of the box, England manager Fabio Capello's shot was cruelly deflected past Bobby Clark. Juventus were in total control and Willie Young, the Dons centre-half, was taken off by the Dons as his tormentor Anastasi was giving the young Don a torrid time. Indeed, the Juve striker had the ball in the net again late on, but was ruled offside. The Dons could count themselves lucky as they escaped with only a two-goal defeat. They had been taught a football lesson.

LOST LUGGAGE

When Aberdeen clinched their first league title in 1955 at Clyde's Shawfield ground, there was little or no celebrations on the field as news filtered through that results elsewhere confirmed Aberdeen as champions. A few celebratory drinks in the dressing room led to some high jinks on the rail journey home. The players were confined to one compartment of the train and Dons keeper Fred Martin found himself taking refuge in one of the luggage racks above the seats. There was also no great welcome in Aberdeen either as around 30 souls waited to welcome the players back to Aberdeen. In the days when cup football attracted all the glamour and success, the Aberdeen squad were presented with the league trophy and medals in an Aberdeen hotel some weeks later.

TO CAP IT ALL

Andy Love was a fast, tricky winger who took over from Alec Reid in the Dons first team in 1925. Signed from Kirkintilloch Rob Roy, Love became a vital supply source for the prolific Benny Yorston, and also weighed in with 83 goals during his Aberdeen career. Love was capped for Scotland in 1931, and was eventually released by the Dons in 1935, when he moved to Aldershot. It was not until 2005 that the SFA recognised around 50 or so previously capped players who were never officially recognised as all of their appearances for Scotland came against foreign nations. Tradition was that only games against the home nations were worthy of being awarded caps. That was changed and Love, as well as the likes of Eddie Turnbull, were belatedly recognised for their efforts.

NINE YEAR WAIT

While Aberdeen's record against Celtic in Glasgow in the 1970s was an impressive one, at Pittodrie it was far more difficult. In March 1975 Billy Williamson was the Aberdeen hero as he scored all three goals in a 3-2 win over Celtic at Pittodrie. Before the match, Aberdeen captain Jim Hermiston shocked the club by announcing that he was leaving at the end of the season to join the police. Williamson completed the Dons win by taking a 78th-minute penalty that beat Latchford to give Aberdeen their first home win over Celtic for nine years.

MATT ARMSTRONG

The spearhead of that formidable Black & Gold side of the 1930s was Matt Armstrong. The statistics on Matt's career reveal a quite remarkable scoring ratio with 155 goals from only 215 appearances, one of the best returns from an Aberdeen striker from any era. At his peak in the mid 1930s, Armstrong also represented Scotland against Germany, Wales and Ireland and he also represented the Scottish League against England and Ireland. Armstrong was also the Aberdeen centre forward for the club's first-ever Scottish Cup final in 1937, going down 2-1 to Celtic. Hampden held a club record crowd of 146,433 that day and it was Matt Armstrong who scored the Dons goal. A native of Newton Stewart, Matt Armstrong was provisionally signed for Celtic in 1930 when he was attracting attention as a free-scoring forward with Port Glasgow Juniors. However, the Parkhead club failed to take up their option and Aberdeen manager Pat Travers stepped in to take him to Pittodrie. As an understudy to the legendary Benny Yorston and latterly Paddy Moore, Armstrong had to bide his time before establishing himself in the Aberdeen first team. When Moore left to return to his native Ireland, Aberdeen turned to Armstrong to take over as the main striker. In the opening game of the 1933/34 season, Matt scored five of the Dons goals in an 8-0 rout of Ayr United and a year later Armstrong was the top scorer with 39 goals from only 43 competitive games. During that season Aberdeen defeated Celtic for the first time in the Scottish Cup; the Dons 3-1 win before a then-record crowd of 40,105 remains one of the Dons' greatest ever performances at Pittodrie. The outbreak of war in 1939 put a hold on his remarkable career and during the subsequent war years Matt guested for Chelsea and West Bromwich Albion, among others, before returning to Pittodrie for one season in 1946 after being demobbed. A short spell in Dumfries with Queen of the South preceded a return to the north where he took up a post as player-manager with Elgin City for the final three years of his playing career. In 1952 he set a Highland League scoring record at the age of 42. Matt Armstrong returned to the Aberdeen area after his playing days and took up employment with SMT garage in Aberdeen. Latterly, he returned to Pittodrie to run the successful club pools in the 1970s. Matt Armstrong passed away after a lengthy illness on October 4th 1995, at the age of 83.

THE BIG 50

Before the start of season 1950/51, Aberdeen had more than 50 signed players following a hectic summer in the transfer market. Aberdeen boss Dave Halliday was in the process of rebuilding the Dons side after the cup winning team of 1947 was all but dismantled.

8 OUT OF 17 FOR BOBBY

Bobby Clark became the club's most capped player when he turned out for Scotland against Denmark in Copenhagen in 1971. Clark earned his eighth cap in the Idraetspark Stadium to overtake Jock Hutton's seven-cap haul from 1926. Clark went on to make 17 appearances for Scotland during his Aberdeen career. Willie Miller broke that record against Brazil in the 1982 World Cup.

NO HAPPY RETURNS FOR JOCK

Happy days for Aberdeen in 1983… As European Cup Winners' Cup holders, the Dons stood on the threshold of becoming the first Scottish team to win the Super Cup. Days before the visit of Rangers, the club was also voted as the best team in Europe for 1983. Aberdeen were also well ahead in the league race by the time a troubled Rangers side came north in November 1983. The Gers were struggling to keep in touch with the Dons and only two weeks before the game they had tried to lure Alex Ferguson away from the Dons to take over at Ibrox. Fergie refused and signed a new deal with the Dons, as did Dundee United boss Jim McLean, who also turned down the Ibrox hotseat. It was third choice Jock Wallace who eventually took over and his first game in charge was against the Dons at Pittodrie. Wallace was hailed as some kind of messiah by the Ibrox legions and he duly took his bow with hundreds of Rangers fans locked outside the ground. Once the euphoria had settled down, the Dons proceeded to take Rangers apart with a display of pace and power that should have yielded more than their three goals. In the opening salvo, Neil Simpson and John Hewitt scored in the first ten minutes to put a masterful Aberdeen in control. The icing on the Dons cake was provided by substitute Ian Porteous who hit a 30-yard screamer past McCloy in the 69th minute.

IAN DONALD

Ian Donald took over as Aberdeen chairman in the New Year of 1994, following the family tradition, after his father Dick Donald died on Hogmanay. It was a natural progression for Ian whose father had played for the Dons in the 1920s before returning to join the Aberdeen board in 1946. Dick Donald took over as chairman in 1970 and he presided over the club's greatest era, and along with Charles Forbes and Chris Anderson, was behind the decision to take Alex Ferguson to Pittodrie – and all the success that followed. The stadium was gradually improved and Ian Donald was around to learn from his mentors following a football career that began with such promise at Old Trafford. Ian also had a spell with Arbroath before joining the Aberdeen board as vice-chairman in 1980. His career in professional football, and his business acumen gleaned from his family business, made Ian Donald an ideal and invaluable member of the Aberdeen board. Ian started out at the age of 12 with Banks O'Dee and a promising career looked assured after playing for Scotland schoolboys in a 2-0 win over England at Wembley before a staggering 92,000 crowd. Ian captained the side at under-15 level and also played at under-18 level. At the tender age of 17 he was on his way to Old Trafford and despite being with Manchester United for more than four years he had to bide his time before making his first team debut against Portsmouth in an English League Cup tie. His career took a turn for the worse when a bad knee injury effectively ended his playing days. During his reign as chairman it is fair to say that Ian Donald has presided over the most difficult period in Aberdeen Football Club history. In the immediate aftermath of the club's halcyon period in the 1980s, it was a tough act to follow. As the game changed beyond all recognition both on and off the field, with finance becoming the most important factor, there was never going to be an easy route. Despite fending off some criticism from the supporters on occasion, Ian Donald continued to serve Aberdeen with distinction. A supporter first and foremost, Ian will still serve the club in his new role as honorary president, still championing the cause.

GOAL RUSH

Seven goals were scored in the first 20 minutes in an incredible opening spell as Aberdeen played Hearts at Pittodrie in November 1926. Aberdeen went on to win 6-5.

AUF WIEDERSEHEN MR EDGAR

Nostalgia was in the air, as well as the German Zeppelin, in 1914/15 when Aberdeen played a former Aberdeen XI in John Edgar's benefit game. Not surprisingly, given the events in Europe at that time, a poor crowd turned out to honour the Aberdeen veteran.

AGE IS NO BARRIER

Donald Colman remains the oldest Aberdeen player to be capped by his country. The legendary full-back made his first Scotland appearance against Wales at Ninian Park in March 1911 at the age of 33. Colman went on to play on four occasions for his country.

FORREST RECORD BUY

When Aberdeen paid £25,000 to Preston North End for Jim Forrest in 1968, he became the club's record signing. The former Rangers striker went on to play for Scotland during his five-year spell at Pittodrie.

FORTRESS PITTODRIE

Season 1929/30 heralded the beginning of better days for Aberdeen when they became the only side in Britain that season to go through the whole campaign undefeated at home. The 21 matches yielded 62 goals.

AWAY DAY BLUES FOR DONS

Season 1930/31, Aberdeen's league campaign was blighted by inconsistency. At Pittodrie, they recorded wins over Clyde (8-1), Dundee (6-1) and Hibs (7-0). But, on their travels, lost 5-0 at Motherwell and 4-0 at Rangers.

PLAYING FOR KEEPS

An injury jinx at the start of season 1956/57 struck two Aberdeen keepers. Deputy keeper Reg Morrison, who dislocated a finger in a pre-match warm up before a game against Celtic, swiftly followed Fred Martin's broken finger during a friendly. With no sub allowed, Morrison bravely played on.

500 UP FOR ABERDEEN

Without doubt one of the most important goals ever scored by Aberdeen in the Scottish Cup also marked a definitive landmark in club history. Joe Harper's penalty against Celtic at Hampden in April 1970 was also the Dons' 500th goal in the national competition. It was that historic penalty that paved the way for a famous 3-1 Aberdeen win over a much-vaunted Celtic side that could do little wrong at the time. It fell upon Joe Harper, the undisputed 'King' of Pittodrie, to claim the Dons' 500th. Not many outside of Pittodrie gave the Dons much hope of taking anything from Celtic but it was Harper's goal that set up the win and it was also a tactical triumph for boss Eddie Turnbull. Joe, who recently was recognised with six more goals from other matches, which took him above the 200 mark for the Dons, takes up the story; "Yes, it was a tactical thing between Eddie and the team. He made sure that we had pace on each flank with Jim Forrest and Arthur Graham. He told me that we had to get in behind them and exploit their defence. Just sit in, he told me, and draw them out. It worked a treat. I remember the second goal when I turned Billy McNeill and sent Jim Forrest away. Jim set up Derek for the goal. It was the first time I had been involved in anything tactical like that – Turnbull was a genius at that. Going back to the penalty, I remember that the Celtic players tried to keep the ball while the arguments went on. It took around 7-8 minutes before I was able to take the kick. I eventually got the ball back and started playing keepy-up with it. It might have looked arrogant but I was trying to compose myself really. When I got down to taking the kick I have always been a firm believer in placing the ball. The best ones were when I would go in at an angle and hit the ball low to the other corner. It worked perfectly. Williams was going the other way and could do nothing about it. It was close though, as it was just inside the post. I remember a reporter asking me after the game what was going through my head at the time, was I the brash young striker? No, I said. All I was thinking about was that if I scored and we won the cup I could get any girl in Aberdeen that night!"

COVER UP

Aberdeen installed seating at the front of the Main Stand at Pittodrie in the summer of 1968 as the old enclosure was replaced with the new seats. At that time the club also had ambitious plans to erect a cantilever stand over the South Terrace. The club decided that the cost of £200,000 was excessive, and the plans were shelved. At that time, the only two grounds in Britain that had cantilever stands were Hillsborough and Molineux. The club eventually went on to develop the ground and the South Stand was covered in 1980.

ST. MUNGO

Aberdeen lost out in the final of the St. Mungo Cup in 1951; a one-off tournament which was part of the Festival of Britain and was primarily based in Glasgow. The Dons had seen off Rangers and St Mirren before clashing with Hibernian in the semi-final. A 1-1 draw at Celtic Park preceded a 2-1 Pittodrie win. An 80,000 crowd at Hampden witnessed the Dons go down 3-2 to Celtic in controversial circumstances in the final after they had swept in to a two-goal lead.

UNITED HONOUR TO DONS

Manchester United have provided the opposition for two Aberdeen stalwarts of different eras in testimonial matches. United visited Pittodrie in 1925 to honour Bert MacLachlan, while Alex Ferguson returned with his side on the verge of a unique treble in 1999 to pay tribute to Dons kit man Teddy Scott. United returned in July 2008 to mark the 25th anniversary of the Dons' Gothenburg success in the 1983 European Cup Winners' Cup.

314 AND OUT FOR ALLY

Aberdeen full-back Ally Shewan made a club record 314 consecutive first team appearances before a dispute with the club resulted in Dons boss Eddie Turnbull leaving the veteran defender out of the side in 1969. During that spell, Shewan captained the Dons for the day against Motherwell on March 23rd 1967 to mark his 250th consecutive appearance.

THE BLACK & GOLD

Not since their formation in 1903 had Aberdeen been as close to success as they came in the mid-1930s when the greatest Aberdeen pre-war side reached the 1937 Scottish Cup Final. Following the departure of several established players in the betting scandal of 1931, the likes of Willie Mills, Matt Armstrong, Paddy Moore, Eddie Falloon, Charlie McGill and Jackie Benyon emerged in the side. Armstrong and Mills developed a telepathic understanding that was feared across the country. However, it was not just in attack that Aberdeen looked so impressive; in defence they had the emergence of the Smith, Cooper and McGill trio, following on from some sound defensive partnerships in previous years. Bob Fraser was the captain and alongside him was Irishman Eddie Falloon, one of the smallest central defenders ever to grace Pittodrie. It was in the 1935/36 season that Aberdeen went so close to landing their first championship. A third-place finish does not tell the true story. Aberdeen had looked champions right up until an incredible 2-1 defeat at lowly Arbroath. Such a slip up at that time was often crucial and although 26 of their 38 games were won it was still not good enough to take the title. It was the year that Aberdeen embarked on regular scoring sprees, averaging almost three goals a game. In 1937 the Dons went one better and finished as runners-up in the league, and finalists in the Scottish Cup. Talk of an unprecedented double was common and it was not until the closing weeks of the race that Aberdeen fell at the last hurdle. It was heartbreaking stuff and it remains ironic that such a great side were destined never to win the club's first major trophy. The cup final at Hampden that year, of course, attracted the British record crowd of 146,433, such was the attraction of this Aberdeen team. Confidence had never been so high going into the final; on paper Aberdeen were the more potent combine and Celtic had little flair to compete with the Aberdeen players. It all went sadly wrong for the Dons as players like Willie Mills never reached the high standards they had set and it all ended in bitter disappointment. By 1939 the team that had came so close was beginning to break up and the declaration of war that year brought down the curtain on an era that had promised so much.

FRANK ON FIRE

Frank McDougall scored in eight consecutive league games for the Dons in the 1984/85 season as Aberdeen went on to retain their league title. McDougall ended as top scorer in the Scottish Premier in his first season with Aberdeen after his £100,000 transfer from St Mirren.

FAIRS FAIR FOR DONS

On the final day of season 1966/67, Aberdeen defeated Rangers 3-2 at Ibrox to deny the Glasgow club of the league championship with virtually the last kick of the season. The memorable win also clinched a Fairs Cup place for the Dons and a first crack at European football.

BONUS ROW

When Aberdeen won the league title in 1955, they were among the best-paid players in British football, commanding up to £22 per week in wages. With the English league still having a wages limit in place, the top Scottish clubs were able to break it which meant that not many top Scottish players left the country in the 1950s. Aberdeen were also due additional money for winning the title. The mandatory £1,000 came through from the Scottish League as was the usual payment for the winners that would be split amongst the players. However, a delegation led by Jimmy Mitchell and Archie Glen approached the Aberdeen board for more cash which they thought was appropriate after they had won the title. Their argument was a valid one as home crowds were up and cup runs were the norm, so the club certainly cashed in through the additional gate money. The Aberdeen directors were not so forthcoming and the players were told that no more money would be paid out. It left a bad taste after what was a momentous achievement. Days later manager Dave Halliday left to take over at Leicester City.

THEN THERE WERE FIVE

Aberdeen had five different managers during the 1970s, as many as there had been in the preceding 67 years. Eddie Turnbull, Jim Bonthrone, Ally McLeod, Billy McNeill and Alex Ferguson were all appointed during the decade of change.

DREAM COME TRUE FOR PETER

Former Dons winger Peter Weir fulfilled a personal ambition when he signed for the Dons in 1981. Weir became a Dons fan after going to the 1970 final between Aberdeen and Celtic. "My dad took me to watch the 1970 final and I was so impressed by Aberdeen that I decided they were the team for me," said Weir after he completed his dream move to Pittodrie.

SIR ALEX

Alex Ferguson was a surprise choice to take over from Billy McNeill in 1978. After a successful spell with St Mirren which ended in acrimony, Fergie ticked all the Aberdeen boxes; a young and enthusiastic manager making his name in the game and with a burning desire to succeed. While his first season was one of mediocrity, it was the winning of the Premier League title in 1980 that set the tone for seven glorious seasons at Aberdeen. Ferguson presided over ten major trophy wins, including the European successes in 1983. It was Fergie's ability to instil a belief and pride in his players that helped Aberdeen to dominate domestic football in Scotland from 1980 to 1986 before his inevitable departure. That came in November 1986 when Manchester United came calling to Ferguson to resurrect their ailing fortunes. It is at Old Trafford, of course, that Ferguson has laid down a lasting legacy that has made him the most successful manager in British football.

FIRST DEFENCE

Aberdeen's defence of their first Scottish Cup came in the tranquil setting of Crawick Holm, Sanquhar, where the Dons cruised past non-league side Nithsdale Wanderers 5-0 in a second round tie on February 7th 1948. Aberdeen went out in the next round at home to Hibernian in a rare home defeat against the side that the Dons had beaten in the final.

STEPPING DOWN

Dave Shaw had served Aberdeen as a player, captain, trainer and manager during his spell at Pittodrie. In November 1959 he accepted stepping back into his favoured trainer's role as Tommy Pearson was installed as the new Aberdeen manager.

HIGH-FIVE FROM LEGGAT

Graham Leggat was one of the best players ever to emerge from Aberdeen; at a young age he was part of the side that won the title in 1955. Before his transfer to Fulham in 1958, Leggat was renowned for his scoring prowess although he was a right winger during his career. Against Airdrie on October 12th 1957, Leggat scored five of the Dons' six goals in a 6-2 win over the Broomfield side.

SIX OF THE BEST

The Dons recorded their first 100% League Cup group success in 1957 with six wins from their group that also included Queen of the South, Motherwell and Falkirk. This was the first time Aberdeen had won all six matches since the tournament began with the sectional set-up in 1946. The Dons lost out to Clyde in the quarter-final.

SECOND-HALF BLITZ

Whatever manager Jim Bonthrone said to his players at half-time in the Dons League Cup quarter-final against Falkirk, it certainly had a positive effect. The Dons had struggled to break down a stubborn Falkirk defence that included former Don Tom McMillan and a young Stuart Kennedy in what was the first leg of the quarter-final at Pittodrie. It was all change in the second half as Aberdeen blitzed their visitors with eight second-half goals. Joe Harper scored three with Drew Jarvie (2), Jim Forrest, Dave Robb and Arthur Graham completing the rout.

23 AND OUT

Dundee United were the side that eventually ended Aberdeen's iron grip on the Scottish Cup in 1985. After three consecutive cup wins, and 23 games undefeated in the Scottish Cup, Aberdeen went down fighting in a 2-1 defeat against United at Tynecastle on April 17th 1985 in a semi-final replay. A controversial tie was littered with poor refereeing decisions that left Alex Ferguson scathing of the officials after the game. Neale Cooper was also sent off in a game where far worse tackles went unpunished. United's big match jinx struck again though as they went on to lose to Celtic in the final.

PAY AS YOU PLAY?

George Hamilton was a legend at Pittodrie after a memorable career with the Dons. After Aberdeen had won the league in 1955, Hamilton was winding down his career and found himself out of the first team at Pittodrie. That prompted a £2,000 move to Hamilton Academical. The switch did not prove successful and after only three months Hamilton left the club. Typically, he refused to accept wages as he felt that his standards had slipped and did not warrant being paid!

MUIRTON MAYHEM

Perth was the venue for the Dons' Scottish Cup semi-final against Kilmarnock in 1970. The old ground of St. Johnstone was certainly an ideal position for both clubs, but the capacity at Muirton Park was stretched to the limit as a huge following from Aberdeen travelled for the game. While Aberdeen won through in a 1-0 success, trouble flared on the Muirton terraces between the two sets of fans who were packed into the tight terraces. An estimated 18,000 travelled from Aberdeen for the game.

THE TWO BOBBIES

Clashes between certain players have been part and parcel of the game for many years. Personal feuds may not go down well with officialdom but they do make for compulsive viewing. Aberdeen keeper Bobby Clark was a legendary figure around Pittodrie for the best part of 15 years and was highly respected in the game. Strange then that every time Bobby came up against Celtic's Bobby Lennox, there was controversy. It started in 1967 when Lennox clearly took a dive over Clark as the Dons keeper saved at his feet. Clark was incensed when Celtic were awarded a penalty after the Celt's blatant piece of gamesmanship. Worse still was that Clark saved the penalty only for it to be retaken and eventually converted. In later matches Clark began to get the better of Lennox and that clearly had an effect on the Celtic forward. He was prone to punching the ball out of Clark's hands on several occasions. In the 1970 cup final he was at it again, but referees soon got wise to this. Lennox, more than any other player, would stand in front of the Aberdeen keeper in an act of intimidation in the days when such tactics were allowed.

YOU BET?

1931 and the 'Great Mystery' apart, Aberdeen as a club have managed to avoid being embroiled in any such betting scandals that have peppered the game down the years. However, some mischief-making after Aberdeen had surprisingly lost a cup replay against Dundee in 1977 actually instigated a police investigation. As the Dons lost 2-1 to First Division Dundee in a Pittodrie replay, reports emerged that certain Aberdeen players had placed bets on Dundee to win at long odds. The truth was that no big money was won on the outcome of the game and it was all began by some anonymous call to the local paper which led to the fabricated claims.

PROGRAMMED FOR SUCCESS

While Aberdeen may not have been so successful on the field in recent times, their match programme has remained the one to beat in the SPL over the years. The Aberdeen magazine has won the SPL 'title' for being the best match programme in Scotland for the last seven years in a row.

TROPHY FOR THE LOSERS

The 1987 League Cup Final may well have gone down as one of the most dramatic in Hampden history, but it was still devastating for Aberdeen to lose to Rangers after a thrilling penalty shoot-out. It was also Ian Porterfield's best chance to secure a trophy in the immediate aftermath of the successful reign under Alex Ferguson. An incredible final finished 3-3 after extra time. It was Welsh captain Peter Nicholas who missed for the Dons as the cup went to Ibrox. The Scottish League even went to the bother of awarding Aberdeen with a trophy for playing their part in a classic final, although that was no consolation at the time.

ULLEVI STADION...

...the venue in the Swedish port of Gothenburg that remains part of Aberdeen FC folklore. It was at the Ullevi in May 1983 that Aberdeen humbled Real Madrid to lift the European Cup Winners' Cup, the last Scottish club to be successful in Europe.

HEARTLESS REFEREE

Despite the ongoing hostilities in Europe, the Scottish League continued almost unnoticed in 1915. In the closing weeks of the season Aberdeen welcomed Hearts to Pittodrie on April 3rd 1915. The game meant little to Aberdeen but was of the utmost importance to the visitors who were going for the championship. It transpired that the referee failed to turn up so a 'substitute' ref had to be found. As it turned out, Aberdeen took a point off Hearts in a 0-0 draw, a result that had a crucial bearing on the outcome of the title. Hearts appealed to have the game declared null and void and played again, but their appeal was thrown out and Celtic went on to take the title.

VICTORIA UNITED

The team that emerged from the south side of Aberdeen and eventually was part of the amalgamation of the present Aberdeen FC. It was in the summer of 1889 that Victoria began playing and their first game was actually against Celtic. The Victoria Bridge Grounds were opened by a group of cycling enthusiasts and the idea was that multiple sports could be played on the grounds, including football. The facility was certainly one of the best around with a bar, dressing rooms and pavilion all in place with a capacity of around 20,000.

SUITS YOU SIR!

Aberdeen had made steady progress in the Scottish League ever since they were first admitted in 1905 to the top division. At the end of the 1909/10 season a local tailor in King Street rewarded the Aberdeen players' efforts for finishing fourth in the table with the donation of a 'Chanel' suit for each of the first team squad.

A WALTZ FOR STRAUSS

Billy Strauss, the South African winger who enjoyed a memorable Aberdeen career, was awarded a testimonial by Plymouth Argyle, the club he joined after leaving Aberdeen in 1946. Strauss was on target in a 2-2 draw against Aberdeen, who made the long trip to the south coast to honour their former player in May 1951.

UNWANTED TRIPLE FOR DONS

One of the most disappointing finals for Aberdeen was the 1959 Scottish Cup Final. The Dons had the opportunity to end the 1950s in some style with a cup win. After losing the 1953 and 1954 finals to the Old Firm, Aberdeen were favourites to come out on top against St Mirren. However, the Dons simply did not turn up on the day and Hugh Baird's late goal was but a mere consolation for a disappointing Aberdeen in a 3-1 defeat.

DOWN THE CLYDE

One of Aberdeen's lowest post war attendances turned out for the visit of Clyde on April 19th 1975, with only 3,300 bothering to attend in wretched weather, as neither side had much to play for.

TWO'S COMPANY

In June 1988 Aberdeen appointed Alex Smith and Jocky Scott as co-managers in what was a first for the club with a dual appointment into the Pittodrie hotseat. Former player Drew Jarvie was also part of the package as he was installed as assistant manager in the new set-up.

FIRST FOR BIG ECK

The new £4.5m Richard Donald Stand was opened in August 1993 as Clydebank came north for a League Cup tie. Alex McLeish scored the first goal in front of the new stand. Later that month, former European rivals SV Hamburg came across to officially open the new complex, after Princess Anne had visited the new structure for a royal seal of approval.

DONS' FIRST, & LAST, £1M PLAYER

Aberdeen splashed out a club record £1m on Oldham's Scottish international Paul Bernard in September 1995. Aberdeen had been spending huge sums on transfer targets in an attempt to remain at the top of the game in Scotland. It proved to be an expensive exercise that set the club back years in terms of any financial stability. While Bernard was a Scotland international, his hefty salary and transfer fee was never justified.

CHELSEA OUT NUMBERED

Eddie Turnbull, the Aberdeen manager in the 1960s, had been an admirer of the methods used by Scotland's Tommy Docherty when he was Chelsea manager. The Stamford Bridge club travelled north to Pittodrie for a friendly in 1967 and it was Aberdeen that went on to win 2-1 with a late winner from Jimmy Wilson before a 29,000 Pittodrie crowd. Docherty was impressed after watching his team go through a tough time; "Aberdeen were very good, it will take some team to beat them, especially up here." Aberdeen also sported numbers on the front of their strips for the first time, an idea that was brought back from their recent trip to the USA.

17 OUT IN SPRING CLEAN

Not long after taking over as manager at Pittodrie in 1965, new boss Eddie Turnbull was ruthless in his assessment of the squad he inherited as he proceeded to release no less than 17 players in the biggest clear out ever seen at Pittodrie before or since. The biggest casualties were Andy Kerr, who cost £8,000 from Sunderland a year earlier, and former skipper Jimmy Hogg. Eleven of the 17 players were given immediate free transfers with Bobby Hume and Willie McIntosh leaving to go to South Africa.

KR CRUSHED

Amateur side KR Reykjavik were unceremoniously dumped out of the 1967 European Cup Winners' Cup tournament by Aberdeen who registered their record 10-0 win in the preliminary tie. The Icelandic side were then beaten 4-1 in the Reykjavik return. By the time Reykjavik eventually scored against Aberdeen in the 74th minute in Iceland, they were 14-0 behind on aggregate. It was KR inside-forward Hafsteinsson who earned the biggest cheer of the night from the 1,500 crowd as he volleyed past Bobby Clark.

MASON MAGIC

When Paul Mason scored for Aberdeen against Famagusta in a 1990 European Cup Winners' Cup tie in Cyprus, it was the Dons' first away goal in Europe for five years. Aberdeen went on to win 2-0 and went out to Warsaw in the next round.

THE 'WEE MAN'

It was Billy McNeill who took Gordon Strachan to Pittodrie in what has been widely accepted as the best piece of transfer business done by Aberdeen. A fee of £40,000, including Jim Shirra moving to Dens Park, resulted in Strachan joining Aberdeen in November 1977. It was the arrival of Alex Ferguson that also helped Strachan establish himself in the side and he went on to become a vital part of that great Aberdeen side. After winning the Scottish Player of the Year award in 1980, he made his full international debut for Scotland two years later and is another ex-Don in the Scotland Hall of Fame after winning 50 or more caps for his country. Gordon was in the Aberdeen side that won three Scottish Cups in succession as well as the two European trophies that came to Pittodrie in 1983. His final game for the club was the cup final in 1984 after which he moved to Manchester United in a £500,000 transfer that summer. Strachan found further success with United and he was also in the Leeds United side that won the English title in 1992, the last championship before the Premiership began. Strachan was also awarded an OBE in 1993.

DONS 'GIFT' TO UNITED

The friendship between former Aberdeen boss Alex Ferguson and Dundee United manager Jim McLean was well documented. United held on to the coat-tails of Aberdeen in many ways as the Dons broke the Old Firm dominance of the game under Ferguson. While the media christened the eastern uprising under the guise of the 'New Firm', it was Aberdeen who led the way. That was after the Dons effectively gifted United a first-ever trophy in December 1979. Both teams reached the League Cup final that year, but it was Aberdeen who had done the hard task of defeating both Celtic and Rangers along the way. Fate dealt United a helping hand as they did not face Premier League opponents until Aberdeen in the final. The Hampden meeting was dominated by Aberdeen who could just not make the breakthrough against an ultra-defensive United side. In the days when replayed finals were common, the replay was taken to 'neutral' Dens Park which allowed United to muster a crowd. Aberdeen didn't turn up for the final and were deservedly beaten by United who claimed the first national trophy in their history.

SOFIA SO GOOD

In the 1968 Inter Cities Fairs Cup, Aberdeen came away from Sofia with a decent 0-0 draw against Bulgarian side Slavia Sofia. The Dons won the return leg 2-0 to progress. The first game, though, was in doubt for several days before the tie as the Russian invasion of Czechoslovakia meant that there were safety concerns for the travelling Aberdeen party.

DONS TROUNCE BARCELONA!

Not the Spanish champions but the champions of Ecuador no less who were hammered 5-1 by Aberdeen in New York in June 1972. Aberdeen were on a tour of Canada and the US that summer and the exhaustive tour took a toll on the 19 players that made the trip. A crowd of 2,000 turned out at Randall's Island in New York to see Barcelona resort to all kinds of nastiness after Aberdeen had cruised to a four-goal lead after only 24 minutes. Later on that tour the Aberdeen players were attacked on the field by local supporters of Montreal Olympics after Joe Harper scored a penalty against them. The referee took the players off the field and promptly abandoned the game.

AKRANES AND DNIPRO

Icelandic side IA Akranes and Ukrainian outfit Dnipro are the only two sides who have avoided defeat at Pittodrie in a European tie but still went out to the Dons. Akranes drew 1-1 in 1983 in a European Cup Winners' Cup tie, and Aberdeen won the first game in Iceland 3-1. Dnipro drew 0-0 in the 2007 Uefa Cup, but went out after Aberdeen scored in a 1-1 draw in the return.

HEARTS ATTACK

Days after Aberdeen had beaten Hibernian 5-0 at Easter Road to clinch the Premier League title in May 1980, there was a proposal put forward by Hearts to extend the top division to 12 teams with a 'split' midway through the season. It was defeated, which was bad news for the Tynecastle side as they had become something of a yo-yo club with three relegations from the top league in Scotland in the late 1970s and early 1980s.

DON'T LEAVE EARLY!

The wisdom of leaving any game early can be a risky business. Back in 1985, when the Aberdeen youth team were playing Celtic in the final of the Scottish Youth Cup at Pittodrie, one irate supporter left the game with Celtic leading 3-0 and well on their way to the cup as he phoned the local press to complain. An amazing fightback saw the final go to extra time and the young Dons prevailed in a sensational 5-3 win. The supporter's night of misery was completed when he returned to his car to discover he had received a parking ticket! It was on that evening that the entire Aberdeen first-team squad looked on after they had been presented with the league trophy before the game.

RELEGATION FEARS

Aberdeen remain proud of the fact that the club has never been relegated in their entire history. That record was tested in season 1959/60 when the Dons looked doomed; with four games to play they were sitting one place above the bottom in 17th place. In the days of the old 18-team top division, Arbroath were already down and it came down to a straight battle between Aberdeen, Stirling Albion and Airdrie. The crucial game came at Annfield against Stirling on April 16th 1960. Had Aberdeen lost that one, they would almost certainly have been relegated. As it turned out, the Dons won 2-0 and won their final four games of the season to retain their position in the top flight.

FEELING BLUE

The usual tradition of jeering the opposition as they enter the field in time honoured fashion was turned on its head at Pittodrie on November 16th 1968. That was the first occasion that Aberdeen had worn their new change kit of all blue with white socks. Unfamiliar as it was to the home support, when Aberdeen ran out – first to be greeted by a chorus of jeers – it did take a few moments to realise the Dons were playing in blue with opponents Arbroath in their traditional maroon strip. Things did not get much better for the Dons as they had to rely on a late goal from Jim Forrest to save face in a 2-2 draw.

PETER WEIR

After Peter Weir had joined Aberdeen in 1981, many observers claimed that he was the final piece in the Ferguson jigsaw as Aberdeen embarked on a run of success at home and in Europe. Weir was a club record transfer at the time when the Dons paid St Mirren £330,000 for his services with Ian Scanlon going to Love Street as part of the deal. Peter was also a self-confessed Aberdeen supporter from a young age and he was another who had also played for Scotland before his arrival. A winger of great skill with both feet, Weir complemented the Aberdeen midfield and added balance to the left side. Perhaps one for the big occasion, it was Weir who set up Mark McGhee for the winning goal in Gothenburg as he began the move deep inside his own half before beating two Madrid defenders. Arguably, his greatest achievement was his two second-half goals against Uefa Cup holders Ipswich Town at Pittodrie in 1981 as the Dons knocked the holders out in the opening round. Weir was also in majestic form against Hamburg in the Super Cup final in December 1983. Peter Weir eventually joined Leicester City in 1987 after finding himself out of favour with new Aberdeen manager Ian Porterfield.

GERMANS HEDGE THEIR BETS

The biggest scandal to hit German football that eventually saw Hertha Berlin star Zoltan Varga join Aberdeen in 1972 centred on Offenbacher Kickers' last-day problems in season 1970/71. It emerged that Kickers president Horst Canellas had offered Hertha Berlin's players a 140,000DM bung in return for Hertha beating Offenbacher relegation rivals Arminia Bielefeld in the last game of the season. However, Hertha had already agreed a 250,000DM bribe from Arminia to throw the game. Arminia won 1-0. Canellas later published a transcript of a phone conversation with Hertha player Bernd Patzke, and it emerged that match-fixing had been going on for most of that season. An investigation discovered that 18 matches had been rigged and Varga was amongst 52 players who were banned from playing in Germany, which prompted his surprise move to Aberdeen. At that time there were no 'blanket' bans in force which meant the likes of Varga could escape the ban by playing in the Scottish League. Varga was certainly a nomad in football terms as he moved to Ajax after 18 months with Aberdeen.

SEVEN-UP

Jim Bonthrone served East Fife well as a player and the former Aberdeen manager certainly did his bit when the Fifers travelled to Pittodrie on March 3rd 1956. Bonthrone scored all three East Fife goals in the game, the only problem for Jim was that all five Aberdeen forwards helped themselves to goals as the Dons hit seven past a beleaguered Methil defence. Johnny Allan, Bob Wishart, Harry Yorston, Graham Leggat and Jackie Hather were all on target as the Dons ran out 7-3 winners to keep their league challenge going.

DONS JUST CAN'T HACKETT

Ian Porterfield had the most difficult job in football; trying to maintain the high standards set by Alex Ferguson. After Fergie had left the club in November 1986 to begin his Old Trafford dynasty, the club turned to Porterfield as their new manager. In hindsight, it was a near impossible task as Aberdeen begin to slip from the high standards set. What did not help Porterfield was the fact that some of the players he brought in from England were clearly not as good as he had inherited. Gary Hackett, Tom Jones and Keith Edwards were among a host of players brought in to replace the likes of Peter Weir, John Hewitt and Frank McDougall who were all out of favour with the new Aberdeen manager.

LIKE FOR LIKE

While Alex Ferguson was well known for giving youth its opportunity at Pittodrie during his seven-year spell with Aberdeen, in the summer of 1984 he simply brought in direct replacements to supplement his squad, which was certainly not his usual practice. Fergie had lost Gordon Strachan, Mark McGhee and Doug Rougvie after the 1984 Scottish Cup Final win over Celtic, which was their last appearance for the Dons. Ferguson brought in Tom McQueen from Clyde to replace full-back Rougvie and paid St Mirren £100,000 for Frank McDougall who took over McGhee's number nine shirt. Billy Stark was also brought in from St Mirren to take over Strachan's role. That deal was actually completed a year earlier as it was in the summer of 1983 that Strachan told Ferguson that it would be his last season as an Aberdeen player.

LONG TRAIN RUNNING

The troubles that Aberdeen suffered during the Great War were perhaps summed up in the winter of 1917. En route to play Kilmarnock in Ayrshire in January, the Dons travelling party failed to catch a connecting train to the south-west as the Aberdeen train had been delayed. After a lengthy wait at the station, the Aberdeen squad caught the next train to complete their journey. They had to change into their strips on the train and eventually arrived at Rugby Park 25 minutes late. Adding to the Dons' woes they were hammered 7-0 which was a record defeat at that time. A week later, Rangers endured similar difficulties coming north and were beaten 3-1 by Aberdeen before a crowd of 6,000.

KAISER HUMBLED

German legend Franz Beckenbauer was never one for handing out compliments. Indeed, before the Dons were due to play Bayern Munich in Germany in the quarter-final of the European Cup Winners' Cup, Beckenbauer dismissed the Scots. After watching Aberdeen match the mighty Bayern stride for stride on their own patch, Beckenbauer altered his opinion and admitted that he was wrong. German national team boss Jupp Derwall was also impressed; "Aberdeen must be one of the best sides left in Europe. I had heard they were good but I hadn't realised just how good they were. Bayern are the finest technical team in Germany but Aberdeen matched them in every way. I can't remember seeing a Scottish side play so well in Germany." The one man who warned that Aberdeen were a dangerous side was Uli Hoeness; "I told everyone back in Germany that Aberdeen would pose a great threat to Bayern. I said at the time they were better than Barcelona, Inter Milan and Real Madrid."

MCGHEE TOP OF THE EUROS

Current Aberdeen manager Mark McGhee remains the Dons' all-time top scorer in European competition. McGhee scored 14 goals in all European competitions between 1979 and 1984 and included in that haul was a hat-trick against Ujpest Dozsa. McGhee also scored the Dons' first-ever goal in the European Champions Cup against Austria Vienna in 1980.

VARGA GONE, ENTER WILLIE

One Dons 'legend' goes, another arrives. At Cappielow against Morton on April 28th 1973, Zoltan Varga made his final appearance for the Dons before moving on to Ajax, while a young Willie Miller made his first-team debut as a new era at Pittodrie was about to begin.

ERIC BLACK

Joined Aberdeen as an 'S' form signing while still at Alness Academy in 1980 as a youngster of great promise. His first appearance for the club came in Willie Miller's testimonial against Tottenham in 1981 and he also scored on his competitive debut some weeks later against Dundee United. Black formed a lethal partnership with Mark McGhee as the spearhead of the Aberdeen attack. Renowned for his superb heading ability, it was Black whose vital goals brought so much success to the club. Eric opened the scoring in the 1983 European Cup Winners' Cup Final against Real Madrid and he was also on target in the Scottish Cup final against Rangers ten days later. Black left Aberdeen in 1986 after winning a host of winners' medals and he joined French club Metz in a £400,000 deal. A series of injuries curtailed his career and he only made 95 appearances for Metz before being forced to retire at the age of 27. He later embarked on a coaching career and is currently assistant to Steve Bruce at Sunderland in the English Premier League.

CHEAP AT THE PRICE?

A welcome return to competitive action as Aberdeen opened the new season with a 2-0 win over Albion Rovers on August 16th 1919. However, there was a shock for the Aberdeen supporters... admission prices had doubled since the last competitive football during the war in 1917.

TRAVERS TAKES HIS LEAVE

Clyde tempted Aberdeen boss Pat Travers to take over as manager in November 1937. The former Celt went on to help Clyde lift the cup two years later. Travers had been at Pittodrie as a player and manager and led the club to several semi-finals and the Scottish Cup Final in 1937.

ONE IN A HUNDRED

At the end of 1937, Aberdeen were inundated with applications for the manager's job after Pat Travers had announced he was leaving to join Clyde. More than 100 applications were received, one of which was from Dave Halliday, the Scottish player/manager at Yeovil Town. Halliday was the shock choice of the Aberdeen board and he took up his post on January 5th 1938. Halliday delayed his arrival until his side were eliminated from the FA Cup. He had taken his non-league Yeovil Town side to the latter rounds where they eventually fell to Manchester United, despite holding the Old Trafford giants to a 0-0 draw at half-time. Halliday won a treble with the League Cup in 1946, Scottish Cup in 1947 and league title in 1955.

JOHNNY MILLER

Signed from Liverpool for a club record fee on June 8th 1921, Johnny Miller scored on his debut against Ayr United in August and he went on to create a new club-record 23 league goals in his first season. The tally included ten goals in six consecutive league games that season. Miller went on to score 61 goals in 123 games; he was eventually sold to Clyde for £350 in 1927.

MORTON BOGEY

For several years under Alex Ferguson, there was a perception that Aberdeen invariably fell at Cappielow, home of Morton, as they were seen as the Dons' bogey side. While the Dons did indeed suffer some defeats in those matches, the Aberdeen record against Morton was as good as any other side. Morton did end the Dons' 35-game unbeaten league record in 1981, but under Ferguson, Aberdeen did register five wins over the Greenock side at their dilapidated Cappielow ground.

DOUBLING UP

Aberdeen won both league meetings against Rangers for the first time in season 1910/11 with a 4-2 win at Ibrox being followed by a 1-0 win at Pittodrie in December. Aberdeen still lost the league race by four points to their Ibrox rivals. It was the first occasion that Aberdeen had finished as runners-up in the league since they joined the top flight in 1905.

UPS AND DOWNS

Season 1994/95 will go down as a remarkable one in Aberdeen history. It was the year of the great escape as the public address at Pittodrie blasted out the Steve McQueen anthem after Aberdeen had defeated Dundee United 2-1 in the penultimate game of the league season to send United down to the First Division. All the more remarkable was why Aberdeen found themselves cut adrift at the foot of the league for many months. All this and the club could still boast of having four of their squad playing their part in the Scotland side that would qualify for Euro 96. Stewart McKimmie, Duncan Shearer, Eoin Jess and Scott Booth were all capped during that dramatic season.

TWENTY TWENTY

The following ten Aberdeen players have scored 20 or more goals in any league season. Benny Yorston holds the record in the 1929/30 season while Joe Harper is the top scorer of all time.

Johnny Miller	1921/22	23
Bobby Bruce	1926/27	20
Benny Yorston	1928/29	23
Benny Yorston	1929/30	38
Paddy Moore	1932/33	27
Willie Mills	1933/34	28
Matt Armstrong	1934/35	31
Matt Armstrong	1935/36	30
Matt Armstrong	1936/37	24
Billy Strauss	1936/37	24
Joe Harper	1971/72	33
Frank McDougall	1984/85	22
Duncan Shearer	1992/93	22

THREE FOR GEORGE

George Hamilton is the only Aberdeen player who has scored a hat-trick for Scotland in a full international. Hamilton scored his three goals against Belgium in Brussels in the Scots' 5-1 win on May 20th 1951.

PAT WAS THE FIRST

Pat Wilson may not go down as an Aberdeen legend, but the winger made club history when he became the first-ever Aberdeen substitute. After a change in the laws allowed one substitute to 'replace an incapacitated player', Wilson came on for Billy Little during extra time of the Dons League Cup semi-final clash with Rangers at Hampden on October 19th 1966. Ernie Winchester was the first Aberdeen substitute in a league match and he was arguably the very first 'super-sub' as he scored in both matches after coming on against Hibernian and St Mirren later that year.

TEXACO CUP

One of several competitions that emerged in a new era of commercialism but never really got established. Aberdeen only played one tie against Newcastle United in 1974. On September 18th the Dons were held to a 1-1 draw before going down 3-2 in the return at St. James' Park three weeks later.

FOLLOWING FERGIE

Many players who have learned under the guidance of Alex Ferguson through the years have taken on various coaching roles. From the Aberdeen team that won the European Cup Winners' Cup in 1983, most went on to remain in the game. Jim Leighton went on to coach the Scotland and Aberdeen keepers while full-back Doug Rougvie managed Montrose for a spell. John McMaster is still involved with Aberdeen as a scout while Alex McLeish has enjoyed spells with Motherwell, Hibernian, Rangers, Scotland and Birmingham City as manager, alongside former Aberdeen teammate Andy Watson, who was on the bench in Gothenburg. Willie Miller went on to manage Aberdeen, while Neale Cooper is currently manager at Peterhead. Neil Simpson remains part of the current Aberdeen staff, while Gordon Strachan lists Coventry City, Southampton and Celtic on his managerial CV. Peter Weir is another who is still at Aberdeen as chief scout in the west, while Eric Black is a coach with Steve Bruce at Sunderland. John Hewitt had a spell as a manger with Dundalk, while Mark McGhee took over as Aberdeen manager in July 2009. Of the other substitutes in Gothenburg, only Stuart Kennedy and Ian Angus didn't remain in the game after retiring. Reserve keeper Bryan Gunn later became manager at Norwich City.

LUCKY ABERDEEN LIFT CUP

As the only undefeated team in British football that season, it was widely expected that Aberdeen had simply to turn up to defeat St Mirren in the 1955 League Cup Final. However, it was far from easy and it took an outrageous winning goal from Graham Leggat to secure a 2-1 win. Boss Davie Shaw, after the game in true sporting fashion, said his team were lucky but that did not prevent 15,000 turning up to welcome their heroes home.

BEST UNCAPPED FULL-BACKS IN SCOTLAND?

Alex Ferguson once claimed that John McMaster was the best player never to have been capped for Scotland. In the 1920s that accolade would surely have gone to another full-back, Matt Forsyth, who was an outstanding defender for Aberdeen that was never afforded international recognition. In the 1960s, Jimmy Hogg was one of the better Aberdeen players of his generation and one of the most talented. Hogg was another full-back who was never capped for his country despite being outstanding in the red of Aberdeen.

LEAGUE HOPES DASHED

Despite some serious backing from some of the bigger established clubs in Scotland, Aberdeen's hopes of being admitted into the First Division of the Scottish League were dashed on May 10th 1903 at a league meeting. With no application to join the Second Division, Aberdeen would play their first season in the obscure Northern League. It was not until a year later that another attempt failed, but Aberdeen did get admitted to the Second Division at the expense of Ayr Parkhouse.

HAMPDEN HERE WE COME

On April 3rd 1937, Aberdeen reached their first-ever Scottish Cup final after defeating Morton 2-0 at Easter Road. The highly-rated Billy Strauss scored and was injured in the process. It was a watershed moment in Aberdeen history as six previous semi-finals had all ended in defeat. Strauss went on to miss the final due to that injury and he was sorely missed; Strauss had scored in every round of the cup before his injury.

SPANISH INVASION

When Aberdeen qualified for the group stages of the 2007/08 Uefa Cup, the draw threw up some fascinating clashes. One of the games away from Pittodrie was at Atletico Madrid, arch-rivals of Real, the team conquered by Aberdeen in the 1983 European Cup Winners' Cup Final. The tie caught the imagination of the Red Army and despite the Spanish cutting back on their ticket allocation an estimated 8,000 Aberdeen supporters made the trip to the Spanish capital. It was the biggest away support from a Scottish club for a European away tie outside of the Old Firm since the Dons final in 1983. Although the Dons went down 2-0, they did qualify for the latter stages from Group B and went on to face old rivals Bayern Munich in the last 32.

RUNNERS-UP IN 1911

For the first time in their short history, Aberdeen finished in second place in the league in 1910/11, after a memorable season that brought the club so close to a first major honour. It was not until the closing weeks of the season that Aberdeen dropped points in drawn matches against Partick and Hibernian to allow Rangers to take the title. There was more disappointment in the Scottish Cup as Aberdeen fell to Celtic in the semi-final. However, the club did break some new records with Angus McIntosh's 16 league-goal haul setting a new record for the club. Aberdeen were also the only side that went the whole season undefeated at home and they set a new points record of 48.

DEBT FREE IN 1928

Not many clubs could ever claim to be debt free, but despite moderate form on the field, back in 1928, Aberdeen were certainly showing a healthy bank balance. Since the dark days of the Great War when the club almost went out of business, they battled back to become debt free by 1928. Aberdeen raked in more than £30,000 – taken in over a ten-year period in transfers – to help balance the books. The club had also completed upgrading the ground with the centre stand now stretching the length of the field. The transfer of Alex Jackson helped pay for the upgrading.

DONS FANS IN MADRID

PELE & SHEARER

In December 2002 Steve 'Pele' Paterson and Duncan Shearer were appointed as the new 'dream team' that took over from Ebbe Skovdahl, who had announced that he would be leaving Aberdeen later that season. It was certainly a time of change at Pittodrie as the club was wrapped up in their centenary celebrations; little went right on the field. Paterson was renowned for his bargain basement prowess in the transfer market, while Duncan Shearer was a legend as a player with the Dons in the early 1990s. Paterson had been with Manchester United as a youngster and it was his ability to work under a tight budget at Inverness Caley Thistle that prompted Aberdeen's move to take him to Pittodrie. However, with the club cutting costs at every turn, Paterson was never afforded anything like the budgets of his predecessors and after a disastrous spell in charge, Paterson had to suffer the humiliation of leaving Pittodrie in the boot of an official's car to escape the waiting media following his dismissal in 2004. Both Paterson and Shearer returned to the Highland League.

BLOWING IN THE WIND

While it may never seem that important these days, back on April 5th 1947 Aberdeen captain Frank Dunlop won the toss before the start of the 1947 League Cup Final over Rangers. Frank elected to face the gale force wind in the first half, hoping to hold out against their Ibrox rivals. It proved to be a bad choice as Rangers raced into a 3-0 lead by half-time, effectively ending the tie as a contest.

THEO! THEO!

A cult hero from Holland, Theo Snelders was a keeper of great ability who had the difficult task of replacing Jim Leighton in 1988. Snelders was Alex Smith's first signing and Aberdeen paid FC Twente £300,000 for his services. It was on the recommendation of Alex Ferguson who had initially been alerted to Snelders, that Smith paid out the fee without watching the big keeper in action. Snelders was the Dons number one for many seasons, before falling out with Dons boss Roy Aitken at a pre-season photo call. He went on to join Rangers in 1996.

ANGLO SCOTTISH CUP

The ill-fated tournament was introduced for those teams that had failed to make it into European competition. Played between clubs from Scotland and England, Aberdeen, for their part, fared poorly as they were eliminated by Middlesbrough in 1975 and Orient a year later.

HERMY

Jim Hermiston broke into the Dons first team in time to help Aberdeen to glory in the 1970 Scottish Cup after signing from Bonnyrigg in 1965. A fierce competitor at full-back, he could also do a job in the midfield. Hermiston was capped at under-23 level for Scotland and was widely regarded as the best uncapped defender in Scotland at that time. In 1975, as club captain, Hermiston announced his retirement to pursue a career with the police. Hermiston was to emigrate to Australia, where he resumed his football career. Later on he revealed that he stopped playing due to not being selected for the 1974 World Cup finals, despite assurances to the contrary.

CHANGE STRIPS

Aberdeen changed from their traditional black and gold in 1939 to a new red kit which has been their primary colour ever since. Between 1940 and 1965, the first team strip was predominately red shirts with white shorts and apart from a few style changes and subtle flashings, that was not changed much until the start of the 1966/67 season when the Dons sported a complete all-red kit with no real frills. That changed in 1969 when they had two white stripes down the shorts and ever since the Dons have maintained their all-red look.

MILNE HERITAGE

Current Aberdeen chairman Stewart Milne continues in the Pittodrie tradition set out many years ago by two other Milnes. Way back in 1903, when the club came into being, it was Baillie Milne who was an inspirational figure at Pittodrie and the very first chairman of Aberdeen FC. His son Victor Milne went on to play for Aberdeen and he also served Aston Villa and Scotland with distinction.

JESS PERFECT

Eoin Jess emerged from the successful Dons youth side of the late 1980s and shot to fame when he played in the 1989 League Cup Final, helping the Dons to beat Rangers as a raw 19-year-old. Jess was a player of genuine class and he went on to try his luck in the English Premiership with Coventry City, before returning to Pittodrie in a £650,000 move in 1997. Jess was often seen as the shining light in a struggling Dons team. Capped for Scotland 18 times, he was part of the Euro 96 squad. Jess fought his way back after a bad leg fracture in 1992, which curtailed his international promise.

TOM RUDDIMAN FOR GERS

Back in 1905, a young forward by the name of Tom Ruddiman joined Aberdeen from amateur football and contributed so much to Aberdeen's first season in league football, in the Second Division in 1904/05. Aberdeen supporters were then amazed to learn that he had been left out of the side for the new season. As Ruddiman was still an amateur, he was subsequently snapped up by Rangers and he immediately went into the Rangers side that defeated Celtic 3-2, and Ruddiman was offered terms to stay with the Ibrox club.

WILLIAM PHILIP

In 1905, the club appointed William Philip on to the board of directors at Pittodrie. Philip, a master painter, joined the board after Harry Wyllie was installed as chairman. Philip went on to serve Aberdeen as a director until after World War II and his first interest in football was some 60 years earlier as he was associated with Victoria United back in 1888.

TOMMY CRAIG

Tommy Craig was the first Scottish teenager to be transferred for a six-figure fee in British football when he joined Sheffield Wednesday for £100,000 in 1969. A rare talent that was only seen in his formative years at Pittodrie, Craig went on to play for Newcastle United, Aston Villa and Swansea City. Capped for Scotland before moving into coaching, Craig was assistant manager at Pittodrie under Roy Aitken in 1996.

FIRST ST MIRREN VISIT

Paisley club St Mirren first played in Aberdeen away back in November 1892 when they travelled north to face the original Aberdeen in a Scottish Cup tie. The visitors emerged with a thrilling 6-4 victory, but they were given a real time of it by Aberdeen before a big crowd in the tight confines of the Chanonry Grounds. Ironically, St Mirren full-back Crawford who played that day was also in the St Mirren side that visited Aberdeen some 14 years later on league business. Crawford was also in the Scotland side that played Wales in Aberdeen in 1900.

HUTTON IN HIDING

Not many players would relish taking on the burly Jock Hutton when he played for Aberdeen in the 1920s. Hutton was a huge player with a thunderous shot who went on to win an FA Cup medal and play for Scotland. However, Hutton found himself on the wrong end of some crowd abuse at Boghead in Dumbarton in 1920. Bob McDermid, who went on to play for Aberdeen, was involved in a collision with the big Aberdeen defender in the closing minutes. The incident raised the anger of the home supporters who surged on to the field. They took the view that Hutton went in meaning to hurt McDermid and no attempt was made to win the ball. The referee and police managed to clear the area after several minutes while Hutton stayed clear so the game could be concluded. At full-time there was further trouble as hundreds of supporters made it towards the pavilion, still upset at Hutton's actions. Fences were broken down and it was only when police restored order that the Aberdeen players could leave in relative safety.

BIG NIGHT FOR BIG ECK

Alex McLeish was rewarded for his long service to Aberdeen with a testimonial at Pittodrie in December 1988. A capacity 23,000 crowd were treated to an exhibition game between the Aberdeen Gothenburg XI and an international select side. McLeish scored twice in a diplomatic 3-3 draw. Also on show was ageing rock star and former Brentford apprentice Rod Stewart. Kenny Dalglish also played alongside Dons' Jim Bett and Paul Mason in the international select side.

MISSION MADRID

As soon as Aberdeen had booked their place in the 1983 ECWC Final, manager Alex Ferguson was focused on the Dons' final opponents. Fergie went to Madrid to see the return leg of Real Madrid's semi-final with Austria Vienna and saw the Spaniards win through on a 5-3 aggregate. Madrid manager Alfredo Di Stefano had already seen Aberdeen in action as the build up to the final began. Vienna coach Vaclav Halama was in no doubt who would prevail: "Aberdeen for me are a better side than Madrid, even with all of their multi-million pound players." Belgian international boss Guy Thys, who watched Aberdeen eliminate Belgian side Waterschei agreed: "If Aberdeen play anywhere near to what I saw in the first game with Waterschei, they will be too strong for Madrid."

CUP-TIED

Former Aberdeen captain Steve Murray did not enjoy that much success in the Scottish Cup. Murray was the Dons' record signing of £50,000 from Dundee in March 1970. Murray had already played for Dundee in the cup that season, and reached the semi-final before going down to Celtic. That meant the Dons' record buy was ineligible to play in the final. Murray watched from the Hampden stands as Aberdeen went on to win the cup. Three years later Murray was in a familiar position as he watched his new Celtic side in the cup final against Rangers. Murray had just moved from Aberdeen to Parkhead in what was a record buy for Celtic. Again Murray had played for the Dons in the cup earlier that season.

BILLY DODDS

Billy Dodds became the Dons' record buy in the summer of 1994 when Willie Miller paid St. Johnstone £800,000 for his services. Dodds was top scorer with the Dons in each of his four years at Pittodrie. It was his vital goals in May 1995 that helped Aberdeen survive relegation for the first time, and his brace against Rangers in the 1995 League Cup semi-final helped Aberdeen lift the trophy that year. Dodds scored the opening goal in the final against Dundee. Dodds was sold by Alex Miller as part of the Robbie Winters deal and moved to Dundee United in 1998.

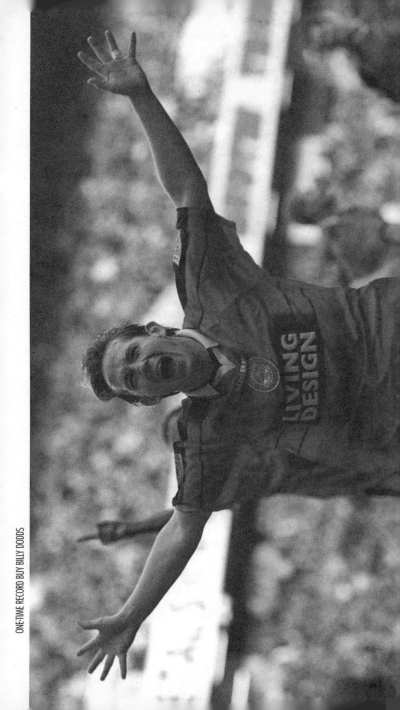

BUMPER

Arthur Graham, or 'Bumper' as he was known by the Dons faithful, shot to fame almost immediately with the Dons. Following his move from Cambuslang Juniors in 1970, Graham played in the Dons side that won the Scottish Cup in 1970, six weeks after making his first-team debut. Capped at under-23 level while at Pittodrie, Graham went on to earn ten caps for Scotland after his suspension from Scotland after the Copenhagen affair in 1975. He was transferred to Leeds United in 1977 for £125,000.

WHITE OUT

Changes in Scottish football back in the 1950s were invariably slow. However, one minor switch that made a huge difference to player and supporter alike was the introduction of a white ball. Aberdeen played with a white ball for the first time in 1951 in a game against Morton. Previously, the older brown leather balls were preferred but with the dark winter afternoons setting in, and in the days before floodlights, the new white balls were an immediate success with both players and supporters.

IT'S A KNOCKOUT!

Aberdeen and Celtic matches are usually one of the most intense fixtures in the Scottish game. After a 1-1 draw at Pittodrie in March 1979, the Dons went to Celtic and won their Scottish Cup replay 2-1 in what was a hostile atmosphere at the Glasgow ground; on and off the field. Trouble broke out between both sets of players at the final whistle as the Aberdeen players celebrated. Aberdeen goalkeeper Bobby Clark was punched as the flare-up continued outside of the dressing rooms.

NITHSDALE MEMORIES

The tiny village of Sanquhar was hit with cup fever when Aberdeen visited in 1948. The tie went largely unnoticed in the north but it evoked memories of previous cup matches, and Nithsdale already had to their credit a victory over 'Aberdeen'. It was back in 1902 that they defeated Orion 1-0 in a Scottish Cup tie although they were defeated 4-0 by Aberdeen at Pittodrie in 1929.

MADRID, COLOGNE OR MANCHESTER?

After Gordon Strachan had told Aberdeen that he would be leaving in the summer of 1984, the transfer speculation intensified in what was his last season at Pittodrie. He was fast becoming the hottest property in Europe and in November 1983 Real Madrid were the latest side interested in signing him as scouts from the Spanish capital watched Strachan on several occasions. The Aberdeen midfielder was also being linked with a number of German clubs. When his eventual move did materialise it was clouded in controversy as Cologne had laid claim to a valid deal that Strachan had signed before he signed for Manchester United. Uefa later fined Aberdeen around £100,000 for their part in the link with Cologne, after the German club lodged an official complaint as they were convinced Strachan had signed for them.

ALEX MILLER

The sight of a certain Alex Miller celebrating a Champions League success under Rafael Benitez at Liverpool must have stuck in the craw with many Aberdeen supporters. Miller's ill-fated spell in charge of Aberdeen did not get off to the best of starts when he was unveiled as the new Aberdeen manager at Pittodrie in 1997. Even before Miller had taken over officially, many supporters' groups questioned his appointment. The former Hibernian manager had gained the reputation of being very dour and defensive and was never one to endear himself to the media. Those fears were realised some 12 months later as Miller was sacked after a series of poor results and questionable signings.

DONS' BEST SIGNING?

Alex Ferguson pulled off a masterstroke in November 1983 by announcing before the start of the Dons' crucial European Cup Winners' Cup tie against Beveren that he was not joining Rangers and that he had signed a new contract with Aberdeen. It was a classic piece of leadership from Ferguson as he received a standing ovation from the crowd before the start and also got the support in the right frame of mind to get behind the team. The game turned into a celebration as Aberdeen cruised past the Belgian league leaders in a 4-1 win to go through to the last eight of the ECWC.

STEVE ARCHIBALD

Steve Archibald was signed by his old boss Billy McNeill from Clyde for £20,000 in 1977. The emerging potential of the striker was to flourish at Pittodrie. Archibald was part of the Aberdeen side that won the Premier League in 1980. His heart was set on a move to England and he was sold for a record £900,000 to Tottenham Hotspur shortly after the Dons' title success. He made his full international debut for Scotland against Portugal during his Pittodrie career. Archibald also went on to play for Barcelona.

CARETAKERS

Former Aberdeen keeper and director George Anderson answered the call when the club was facing going out of business in the tough days of the Great War. Anderson took over team matters at a time of real difficulty. In modern times caretaker managers have steadied the ship, usually in between managerial appointments. Arguably the Dons' first 'caretaker' manager was Harry Melrose who was entrusted to look after the team in the early part of the Dons' 1967 tour to America. With manager Eddie Turnbull unwell and not able to travel, Melrose picked the team for the tour matches. Former player George Murray took over for a couple of weeks in 1975 after Jim Bonthrone left and Ally MacLeod took over. In 1986 Archie Knox stayed on for one game after Ferguson was installed as the new manager at Manchester United. The longest-serving caretaker manager was Paul Hegarty, who filled in for Alex Miller in 1999. Keith Burkinshaw and Gardner Speirs also had brief spells as caretaker managers at Aberdeen.

NORTH AND SOUTH

In December 1939, Tommy Pearson made history when he became the first Scot to play for England. The Newcastle winger had been taking his seat in the stand at St. James' Park when he was summoned by one of the Newcastle directors who told Tommy he was playing for England! Eric Brooks, the regular in the England side, had been delayed in a car crash so Pearson lined up for England and helped them to a 2-1 win. Pearson was later capped for Scotland and also went on to play for Aberdeen in the 1940s.

CLYDE PROTEST

A record 12,000 turned out to see Aberdeen on November 12th 1904 to make it through to the Qualifying Cup final with a 1-0 win. The crowd paid £284, which was not exceeded by the Scotland v Wales international in 1900 due to the increased admission costs. There was plenty of bad feeling towards the Clyde players as they adopted crude tactics to stop Aberdeen and a post-match protest was lodged by the visitors. The SFA threw out the protest some days later.

TRAGEDY OF JACKIE BENYON

Welshman Benyon joined Aberdeen in 1932 from Doncaster Rovers and developed into a quick winger and firm favourite at Pittodrie. He was also in the side that played in the epic 1937 Scottish Cup Final and Jackie provided the cross for Matt Armstrong's goal. Tragedy struck Benyon when he was taken ill on the Dons' tour of South Africa weeks after the final. Benyon went down with peritonitis and died in Johannesburg on June 26th 1937. He was laid to rest in an emotional ceremony in Johannesburg. Sometime later his remains were taken back to be buried in his native Wales.

THE CHEEK OF IT!

Stan Williams' winning goal in the 1947 Scottish Cup Final against Hibernian was often described as a 'goal in a million' and one of pure genius. However, some of the Aberdeen players claimed it was the cheekiest goal they had ever seen and were sure to let Stan know all about it. Williams, of course, scored at Hampden by flicking the ball past the Hibernian keeper at his near post, when everyone else was expecting a cross, such was the angle.

BEST OF IRISH

One of the greatest goals scored at Pittodrie came in November 1937 in an international between Scotland and Ireland. Peter Docherty scored for the Irish in the 14th minute; a goal described by most of the 21,000 crowd as the finest they had ever seen. Docherty hit a ferocious volley from well outside the area that Rangers keeper Dawson did not even react to, such was the quality of the strike.

BELFAST CALLING

Full circle for an Aberdeen and Irish connection. The first Aberdeen player to represent his country was Charlie O'Hagan when he played for Ireland against England in 1907. Some 76 years later, the Dons' largest representation in international football was six, when Jim Leighton, Doug Rougvie, Alex McLeish, Gordon Strachan, Mark McGhee and Peter Weir all played against Northern Ireland in Belfast in 1983. It would have been a magnificent seven had it not been for a rare injury to skipper Willie Miller.

SIX APPEAL

The Dons' biggest representation at under-21 level was six when Bryan Gunn, Neale Cooper, Neil Simpson, Eric Black, John Hewitt and Doug Bell were all named in the squad against Yugoslavia at Pittodrie in 1984.

BLUES FOR EDDIE

Eddie Turnbull was appointed Aberdeen manager in March 1965, and the new boss spent his first three days in the office at Stamford Bridge studying Tommy Docherty's training methods. Turnbull was a new breed of coach making his mark in the game with new methods. Ironically, both Aberdeen and Chelsea won their respective FA Cups in 1970, adding to the fact that both sides won their respective championships for the first time in 1955.

WHITE OUT

In December 1951, Aberdeen played with a white ball for the first time in a league match against Morton at Pittodrie. Early kick-off times in winter did not always mean that matches were played in good daylight. In the days before floodlighting at Pittodrie, it was difficult enough for the players to see the standard brown leather ball, let alone the spectators.

LES BLUES

In April 1987, Scotland played France at Pittodrie in a 'B' international fixture. Included in the French squad was a young Eric Cantona. The Frenchman went on to enjoy a memorable and often controversial career.

TEHRAN CALLING

Not many teams travel to Tehran for a 'friendly' but Aberdeen embarked on a 'world tour' in the summer of 1974 and their first stop was the Iranian capital. The Dons came up against local side Persepolis and were beaten 2-0 in the searing heat before a fanatical home support. The players barely had any time to adjust to the conditions as they played hours after arriving in Iran. Aberdeen went on to tour Australia and New Zealand.

GEORDIE LAD

Alex Mutch, the former Aberdeen goalkeeper, was born in Inverary in 1884. Mutch was also known as Sandy and he made his Aberdeen debut against Hibernian on August 18th 1906. Mutch was transferred to Huddersfield Town in 1910 for a fee of £400 and it was while he was in England that he played in two FA Cup finals in 1920, and again in 1922. Sandy Mutch joined Newcastle United in 1922 for a fee of £850 and went on to become a groundsman with the Geordies for many years after he retired from playing.

NO CUP AT HAMPDEN

The only time that Aberdeen have played in the Scottish Cup final away from Hampden was in 1993. Hampden, at that time, was under reconstruction and was unsuitable to host the game. The Dons lost out to Rangers at Celtic Park in a 2-1 defeat with English-born Lee Richardson scoring the Dons goal. It was Paul Mason's last game for Aberdeen before he completed a £440,000 transfer to Ipswich Town.

COOKING THE BOOKS

Charlie Cooke, the Dons winger and hero of the support, was sold to Dundee in a surprise transfer in December 1964. Although the Dens Park club paid £44,000 for Cooke, the Aberdeen support were convinced that Cooke was sold far too cheaply and to one of the Dons' nearest rivals. The belief was that Cooke was destined to join a big club in England; the move did materialise some two years later when he joined Chelsea, and Aberdeen lost out in a panic measure to balance the books.

100, 200 AND COUNTING

When Aberdeen clashed with Celtic in the semi-final of the Scottish Cup at Hampden in April 1983, there were milestones for two Dons players. Peter Weir, who scored the winning goal, was playing in his 100th game for Aberdeen, while keeper Jim Leighton played his 200th game for the club.

BLINDED BY THE LIGHT?

Before floodlighting became an almost mandatory part of football grounds in Scotland, it was still down to both competing teams to agree to play in matches 'under the lights'. In season 1956/57 Aberdeen refused to play against both Hibernian and Rangers at Easter Road and Ibrox in floodlit matches, citing an unfair advantage would be gained by the home teams. The Dons went on to lose 3-1 at Rangers and 4-1 against Hibernian.

CUP WIN WON OVER PETER

Playing for the team you supported as a boy may be the dream of many an aspiring young player. One such instance that came to fruition was when Peter Weir joined Aberdeen in 1981 in what was a record Scottish transfer back then. Peter first saw Aberdeen in the 1970 Scottish Cup Final when his father took him to Hampden to see the Dons beat Celtic 3-1. "My dad took me across from Paisley and I was so impressed by Aberdeen that day I decided they were the team for me." Weir went on to play his part in the Dons' most successful era in the 1980s.

CAPTAIN DROPPED

In an age when the difficult matter of dropping players was handled with more dignity than we see in the modern game, the original Aberdeen FC captain, Mr J. H. Haise became the first player to be dropped by the new club shortly after its foundation in 1881. Prior to their first-ever game, an announcement was made: "At a committee meeting held in the Albert Hall it was unanimously agreed that the captain seemed uncomfortable with his position on the field, and that an opportunity be afforded him to resign his position; for the benefit of both player and club." There was no messing back then!

DONS STORM THE PALACE

Old Dons favourite Charlie Cooke returned to Pittodrie in January 1973 with his new club Crystal Palace for a friendly. Once again, Aberdeen showed why they had not lost to an English side for 12 years with a convincing 2-0 win before a 16,000 crowd. Cooke was seen as the jewel in the Dons crown in 1961 when he broke through to the first team and was sold some four years later. All attentions were focused on Charlie as he took to the field with a rousing reception from the Aberdeen support.

BRIAN MOORE

Legendary ITV commentator Brian Moore barely knew where Aberdeen was back in 1981 but he soon became familiar with the place, and Pittodrie. Moore was with the ITV team that covered both legs of the Dons' 1981 Uefa Cup tie against Ipswich Town and commentated on several big matches at Pittodrie over the next few seasons as ITV picked up live coverage of some of the great European occasions at Aberdeen. Moore also did the commentary for the Dons' 1983 European Cup Winners' Cup Final for English viewers in the various ITV regions.

RECORD CROWD AT THE GLEBE

Brechin City's tiny ground at Glebe Park may be better known for the huge distinctive hedge that stretches down the perimeter of part of the stadium but back in February 1973, the visit of Aberdeen attracted a record crowd as 8,123 fans crammed in for the Dons' Scottish Cup tie. Aberdeen went on to win a bruising encounter 4-2. Many fans that could not get tickets were seen to use the famous hedge as a means of gaining entry to the ground by unorthodox methods.

BP JAUNT

It is not too often that Scottish clubs visit Egypt. Back in the winter of 1984, Aberdeen went to Cairo for a week's training – and to escape the Scottish winter. Manager Alex Ferguson was delighted to see his players training in ideal weather conditions. The trip was sponsored by oil giants BP, who footed the bill for the week-long trip.

STENHOUSEMUIR

The team from Larbert were the Dons' first opponents in 1903 but they were also the side that inflicted on Aberdeen one of their worst results in modern times. On February 4th 1995 it was the end of the road for Willie Miller as manager and a week later under new boss Roy Aitken Aberdeen were knocked out of the Scottish Cup in a 2-0 defeat at Ochilview.

ALL BETTS ARE OFF

Jim Bett was one of the best midfield players to play for the club following his £300,000 switch from Belgian club Lokeren in 1985. After gaining 27 Scotland caps Jim Bett announced after the World Cup finals in 1990 that he was quitting international football. It is fair to suggest that Bett did not always enjoy the best of luck with Scotland. In the 1986 finals in Mexico, he was the only player in the travelling squad not to get any game time. Four years later and playing in an outside-left position that was certainly not his best, but one that manager Andy Roxburgh insisted upon, he was made one of the scapegoats after the defeat to Costa Rica in Italy 1990.

MCGHEE'S FINAL FLURRY

Current Aberdeen manager Mark McGhee's Aberdeen career began and ended with cup finals very much to the fore. It was on March 30th 1979 that Alex Ferguson signed McGhee from Newcastle United, the day before Aberdeen played Rangers in the League Cup final at Hampden. McGhee went to play for the Aberdeen reserves that night against Rangers at Ibrox on the eve of the final and went on to make his first-team debut against Morton four days later. McGhee's final game for Aberdeen was the 1984 Scottish Cup Final against Celtic.

JOCKY OFF

In the immediate aftermath of the Dons' 1991 Uefa Cup home defeat to BK1903 Copenhagen, co-manager Jocky Scott announced that he would be leaving Aberdeen to take up the manager's role at Dunfermline Athletic. That left Alex Smith in charge of team matters at Pittodrie.

OUT OF IBROX

Not many Aberdeen players have found the trail north to Pittodrie from Rangers in the past. The last player the Dons signed from the Ibrox club for a transfer fee was Alex Willoughby in 1969. In 1970, no less than five Aberdeen players were picked up from Rangers, including three ground staff lads as well as Jim Forrest who was with Rangers before joining Aberdeen from Preston North End.

SUPER ALLY

Ally MacLeod joined Aberdeen in November 1975 from Ayr United after Jim Bonthrone resigned as manager of the Dons. In what was the first-ever season of the 10-team Premier League, McLeod took over at Pittodrie when Aberdeen were struggling in ninth place. Despite back-to-back wins over Rangers – including the first at home for ten years – and Celtic in December 1975, the Dons' survival was not secured until the final game of the season against Hibernian at Pittodrie. In the summer of 1976 MacLeod set about turning the Dons' fortunes around and he had already brought back Joe Harper in April when he signed Stuart Kennedy from Falkirk and Dom Sullivan from Clyde. MacLeod had promised the Aberdeen support a trophy within a year and he duly delivered in November 1976 when Aberdeen beat Celtic 2-1 at Hampden to lift the League Cup in what was Willie Miller's first trophy as Dons captain. Following the departure of Willie Ormond from the Scotland job, MacLeod was asked by the SFA to take over the national side. Ally MacLeod left Pittodrie in May 1977 to take up his new position. Ally presided over a disastrous World Cup campaign in Argentina in 1978 and returned to club management with Ayr United, Motherwell and Airdrie. As a player, MacLeod was with Third Lanark, Blackburn Rovers and Hibernian before a move to Ayr as player-coach. MacLeod's highlight from his playing days was a Wembley appearance for Blackburn against Wolves in the 1960 FA Cup Final.

Aberdeen record under Ally MacLeod

	P	W	D	L	F	A
1975/76	27	9	8	10	38	34
1976/77	50	26	13	11	80	52
Total	77	35	21	21	118	86

NO HAMPDEN HEARTACHE FOR DONS

Despite Hearts missing out on the title seven days earlier, it was Aberdeen who were still seen as the team to beat when the sides met in the 1986 Scottish Cup Final. Aberdeen manager Alex Ferguson said before the game that he expected his side to impose themselves on the match and take full advantage of their experience of the big occasion. He knew Hearts would be nervous and if Aberdeen hit them hard in the opening exchanges it could well set the tone for the game. What was also significant was that Hearts had thrown away the league title only seven days before the final. Hearts had to avoid defeat at Dens Park on the final day to win the title. It all seemed so straightforward but when Albert Kidd scored a late goal for Dundee to make it 2-0, the Hearts dream was over. It was a hammer blow for the Tynecastle side and this was not lost on Ferguson whose mind-game psychology was not even required in the lead-up to the final. Not unlike the Dons' earlier League Cup win over Hibernian that season, it was Aberdeen who imposed themselves on the game in the opening exchanges. Within five minutes, a probing run by John Hewitt allowed the Dons winger to cut in from the right. Hewitt enjoyed the freedom of Hampden as the Hearts defence backed off. It was a crucial error as Hewitt hit a shot into the corner of the net from 20 yards. Hewitt was possibly not even a definite for a starting place as Ferguson dropped striker Eric Black after it emerged that he had agreed a move to French club Metz after the final. Hearts came back into the game but after John Robertson's lob came back off Jim Leighton's bar, as so often in the past Aberdeen made the Jambos pay a heavy price. Three minutes after the restart Aberdeen hit Hearts with a second goal of pure class. Peter Weir had been giving Hearts captain Walter Kidd a torrid time all afternoon and when Frank McDougall cleverly dummied Weir's cross, Hewitt ghosted in to give Henry Smith no chance. From that point on, Aberdeen tortured a Hearts side that were clearly crestfallen. There was further dismay in the 75th minute when Billy Stark completed the scoring. The final ignominy for Hearts came shortly after when captain Walter Kidd was sent off after a disgraceful show of pettiness; the defender threw the ball into Peter Weir's face after the Dons winger had once again glided past him.

REFEREE IN THE WAY

Scottish referee J. B. Stevenson would probably not care to remember the Dons clash with Dundee at Dens Park on New Year's Day 1924. He got a bit close to the action on one occasion and ended up being flattened by a wayward kick in the heat of the action. Much to the amusement of the huge crowd, Stevenson boldly limped on for the rest of the game.

GERMANY CALLING

By tradition, Aberdeen as a club in their formative years were always keen to travel abroad on tour. While most countries would guarantee their costs, Aberdeen were the first British club to tour Eastern Europe in 1911 and they also embarked on a short tour of Germany in May 1924. Ironically, the Dons also played English side Bolton Wanderers in Leipzig on May 18th, losing 3-1. The club announced that they returned from the short tour with a profit of £380 for their troubles.

ONE WAY TICKET

In July 1924, Aberdeen announced they were signing brothers Walter and Alec Jackson, who had been playing in America, although both were Scottish-born. Alec Jackson went on to fame with Scotland. Both had been star performers for the Bethlehem Steel Works side in America, widely regarded as the best team in the States. The signing process was initiated by Jimmy Philip before he announced he was standing down as Aberdeen manager that year. Pat Travers completed the deal to take both to Pittodrie. One footnote was that Alec retained one half of his ticket back to the USA for many years. Such was his popularity in the States, the owner of the Steel Works told him that his job would always be open for him.

STEWART DAVIDSON...

...joined Aberdeen as a promising winger and took some time to establish himself in the first team. Emerging as a formidable defender, his 20-year association with the club was broken by the First World War. After a spell with Middlesbrough, Davidson moved into coaching and was assistant manager of Chelsea between 1939 and 1957.

1983 EUROPEAN CUP WINNERS' CUP FINAL

Aberdeen v Real Madrid – The Big Match Stats

Aberdeen		Real Madrid
7	Shots on Target	3
4	Headers on Target	0
3	Shots off Target	6
4	Headers off Target	3
22	Free Kicks	20
4	Corners	5
2	Goals	1
59%	Possession	41%

Aberdeen had to play a preliminary tie on their way to the final, although Swiss side Sion offered little resistance as they were beaten 11-1 on aggregate. Real Madrid reached the final against the Dons after beating Romanian side Baia Mare (5-2), Ujpest Dozsa (4-1), Inter Milan (3-2) and Austria Vienna (5-3). Aberdeen only lost one game in the whole competition, a 1-0 defeat in Genk to Waterschei after Aberdeen had taken a 5-1 first leg lead across to Belgium.

THEY SAID IT; GOTHENBURG 1983

"The players fulfilled their promise to the club's magnificent support not only by their performances but in the style in which they achieved so much. We, as a board, pay tribute to the players and supporters of Aberdeen who did us so proud."

Dick Donald, Aberdeen chairman on the flight home to Aberdeen

"The first aircraft came in at 5.20am and was out again at 6am. By 2pm we had all 28 flights to Sweden on the day of the final away from Aberdeen."

Roland Gunn, commercial manager at Aberdeen Airport.

"Gothenburg was our big moment and we did it for Aberdeen fans everywhere, everything else was a side issue."

Alex Ferguson, Aberdeen FC manager in reflective mood on the flight home.

"It was our biggest ever movement of our goods. We were well stocked up and coped with demand, but the wine and champagne sales surprised us."

Louis Cowe, manager of the duty-free shop at Aberdeen Airport.

"Aberdeen have what money can't buy – a soul; a team spirit built in a family tradition."

Real Madrid manager Alfredo Di Stefano after losing to Aberdeen in the final.

"This House warmly congratulates Aberdeen FC on their outstanding achievement in winning the Cup Winners' Cup, and believes the manner of their victory reflects great credit on the players and management of the club, on the supporters and on the whole of football in Britain."

Message received from the House of Commons the morning after the final.

"Congratulations you have done us proud. Well done to you and the boys, keep up the good work."

Liverpool manager Bob Paisley sent his best wishes with a telegram.

"Aberdeen deserved their victory; they are one of Europe's top teams now. I was looking forward to the game going to penalties but my players wanted to win. That was a mistake because Aberdeen were the stronger side in the conditions."

Alfredo Di Stefano at the after-match press conference.

"I was delighted to learn of Aberdeen's splendid victory and send my congratulations to all concerned."

The Queen Mother in a message sent to the Aberdeen Lord Provost.

"Our homecoming after Gothenburg was the high point of my life. The flags and banners with our bus nosing its way through tens of thousands of people sent the blood tingling."

Aberdeen maestro Gordon Strachan on the team's return to Aberdeen.

PREMIER LANDMARKS

Drew Jarvie had the honour of scoring the Dons' 100th goal in the Premier League when he scored against Celtic at Parkhead on April 20th 1977. John McMaster notched the club's 500th Premier goal when he scored in the Dons' 5-0 rout of Kilmarnock at Pittodrie on May 5th 1983. The Aberdeen squad were in the final preparations for their next outing which was the European Cup Winners' Cup final meeting with Real Madrid in Gothenburg. Scott Booth had the distinction of scoring the Dons' 1,000th Premier League goal in the 5-0 win over Hearts on February 2nd 1991. Eoin Jess scored goal number 1,500 in the game against Dundee United at Tannadice on September 23rd 2000. The most points Aberdeen have managed in a Premier League season was 65 in 2007 which was only good enough for a third-place finish. In the days before three points were awarded for a win, Aberdeen managed a 64-point haul in 1992/93 that was still short of Rangers' total in what was Willie Miller's first full season in charge at Aberdeen. Miller became the first Aberdeen player to play in 100 Premier games when he led the Dons out against Clydebank on March 21st 1978. When Aberdeen won the championship in 1985 they won 27 of their 36 league games. In 1994, Aberdeen drew 21 of their 44 league matches, the most draws in any season. Aberdeen have never finished in fifth place since the Premier League began in 1975. The Dons have failed to qualify for European football in 12 of the 34 seasons of the Premier League.

POLE-AXED

Friendly fixtures may mean very little in terms of tangible success but back in an age when clubs played for more than pride in these games, one of the most enthralling ever seen at Pittodrie was the Dons' 5-0 hammering of Polish side Gornik Zabrze in 1970. Knocked out of Europe by Honved earlier in the season, Gornik were Polish cup holders and on their way to reaching the European Cup Winners' Cup final. Aberdeen displayed all the power and passion required to destroy the once slick Poles. Aberdeen were in a rich vein of form and in the middle of their record-breaking sequence of games without conceding a goal. The only 'shock' of the evening was that for once Joe Harper was not among the scorers.

ATTACK TO DEFENCE

December 1972 was well known as the time that the club sold star player and idol Joe Harper to Everton in a record £172,000 deal. It was also at that time that Aberdeen made a switch that was to be a crucial factor in their history. Under Teddy Scott, the Aberdeen 'A' team was struggling for central defenders for a game against Rangers at Pittodrie. Young Willie Miller was withdrawn from his original striking role and put in as a centre-half, along with Billy Williamson, in what was a makeshift defence. Aberdeen went on to win 2-0 and Miller was soon deployed in a defensive position he was to make his own for the best part of 20 years.

BIBLIOGRAPHY

Aberdeen: A Centenary History 2003
Kevin Stirling, Desert Island Books (2002)

Aberdeen: Champions of Scotland 1955
Kevin Stirling, Desert Island Books (2002)

Aberdeen City Libraries Archive

Aberdeen Journals Library